'We need good cheer and happiness, hope and love. The uglier, older, meaner, iller, poorer I get, the more I wish to take my revenge by doing brilliant colour, well arranged, resplendent.'

Vincent van Gogh in Arles, France, 1889

Atmosfloric

Flower colour in home and garden

SEAN A. PRITCHARD

MITCHELL BEAZLEY

Contents

Pursuing a Mood: *The Emotion of Flower Colour* 8
Combining Flower Colour 14

Atmosphere 1: *Romantic* 39
Atmosphere 2: *Energetic* 97
Atmosphere 3: *Reflective* 159

Atmosfloric: *Escaping with Flower Colour* 217

Index 220
Acknowledgements 223

Page 2: A simple display of common marigolds (*Calendula officinalis*) at Tilley Printing in Ledbury, Herefordshire, one of the last remaining letterpress printers in the UK. There is something so honest about this kind of orange. Opposite: The kitchen at Charleston, in East Sussex, with the gloss-white of *Narcissus* 'Actaea' shimmering as it catches some welcome spring sunlight.

Pursuing a Mood
The emotion of flower colour

In a garden or cut flower display there are multiple factors that engage the observer in some way. There is the intrigue of scent, the impact of scale and the tactile interest of texture. Yet invariably, perhaps no other sensory element piques our curiosity more so than colour. When I consider the hundreds of gardens I have ever visited, it is the slight quickening of my heartbeat when I walk into a hot border or the sense of restfulness to be found among cool drifts of spring bulbs that I remember first; it is always the colour that remains etched into my memory like a scrapbook of pigmented emotions.

Previous pages: An energetic tulip scheme that includes the cultivars 'Amber Glow', 'Annie Schilder', 'Bronze Perfection', 'Daydream' and 'Orange van Eijk'. Above: A late summer display of dahlias. Opposite: The cobalt of delphiniums is mixed with the icy sky-blue of *Nigella damascena* 'Miss Jekyll' and the ivory cultivar 'Miss Jekyll Alba'.

Each of us has our own idiosyncratic relationship with colour. While basic cues are inherent in all of us (the warning of red, the survival of blue), as we navigate the world we also build increasingly more complex associations that profoundly shape our preferences. This is something psychologists refer to as Ecological Valence Theory: the theory that our past experiences define our fondness or dislike for certain hues. As gardeners and flower arrangers, we are more often than not drawn to colours that reflect pleasant situations or objects from somewhere in the messy and complicated history of our lives – even if we are not always aware that this is what we are doing. Perhaps it is the buttery lemon of a favourite childhood blanket or the sparkling turquoise eyes of a first love: these are all powerful and highly personal biases that over time become ingrained in our subconscious.

But rarely when working with flower colour are we satisfied with just one hue. Most often, our aim is to group colours in such a way that as a collective they heighten a sense of something which is greater than its constituent parts. On the surface, it may seem as if the only principle driving the way flower colour is assembled is one purely based on aesthetics – for example, what shades of red will look most attractive with this type of pink or which kinds of purples will be prettiest with these blues? Yet I would argue that for most gardeners and flower arrangers, there is a motivation lurking beneath the superficial. We are artists chasing abstract and highly individual moods, indulged by a floral world with limitless colour choice. We want to feel moved in some way – to be lifted from the everyday – and we look for stories in the relationships that tints, tones and shades create.

I am reminded often of a passage from Gertrude Jekyll's 1916 book *Annuals and Biennials*:

'What is meant by colour schemes is not merely the putting together of flowers that look well side by side, but the disposition of the plants in complete borders in such a manner that the whole effect together is pictorial.'

Jekyll, for me one of the greatest ever observers of floral nuance, recognized the power that colour groups can have in the garden (and, by extension, the vase) to create evocative and fantastical atmospheres that transport the observer away from the prosaic and predictable routine of day-to-day life. Gardens and flower arrangements should be an escape, sources of intrigue that, if only for the briefest of moments, offer the imagination a chance to run unbridled through a maze of curiosity and extravagance. As with anything visual – painting, photography, film, sculpture – the ways in which one person responds to the atmosphere of flower colour is highly personal. I may pause for a second by a drift of

Below: Steps at Iford Manor, Wiltshire. A green carpet of self-seeded lady's mantle (*Alchemilla mollis*), Mexican fleabane (*Erigeron karvinskianus*) and trailing bellflower (*Campanula poscharskyana*) is combined with a display of blue cornflowers (*Centaurea cyanus*) in a white jug to create a scene that exploits colour to maximum soothing effect.

tulips in lemon-yellow and sunset-orange and be taken to the sensory overload of a raucous carnival, yet the person who comes next may view the same scene with indifference. We each bring our own idiosyncratic view of the world to gardens and floral displays, and it is these quirks of personality that make their creation so endlessly captivating.

To my mind, there are three moods that assemblies of flower colour evoke most successfully. The first, and perhaps the one that I am most often driven by, is a sense of romance. It is the enchanting whimsy of pinks and the never-ending mystery of purples; flowers that soften the edges of everyday life and encourage fanciful daydreams. The second is a feeling of boundless energy. This is a cocktail of reds, yellows and oranges that leap from hot borders and frenzied vases to create moments that motivate with their dizzying and uninhibited lust for life. The third, although by no means the least seductive, is a comforting impression of reflection. These are blues, greens and whites that coalesce to soothe and quieten our often fraught and over-stimulated minds.

In putting together this book, my aim has been to explore these three atmospheres not only through my eyes, but also through the lens of others who have cultivated a close relationship with the decorative potential of flowers. People for whom living and working spaces become opportunities to explore curious dreamworlds – creatives who indulge the whimsical and sometimes erratic whims of their imagination. Although some of these people are professional gardeners, there are others who by day are actors, stylists or painters. These are people who harness the ornamental power of flowers as a happy extension of their downtime, people who have come to find how fulfilling a life lived close to the garden can be. Yet gardener or not, there is an undeniable thread connecting all those who appear in the following pages: the everyday made more atmospheric.

It is worth noting that although in this book specific colours are attributed to the broad atmospheres of romance, energy and reflection, these are not intended to be wholly prescriptive. They represent one view of colour – my own – in a world that is saturated with opinion on the topic. The subject is so vast, and in many ways so personal, that the following pages cannot possibly cover every nuance of science and sentiment. Indeed, for centuries, much has already been written by gardeners, botanists and enthusiasts detailing the intricacies of this complex and enchanting issue.

Opposite: Icelandic poppies (*Oreomecon nudicaulis*) in shades of ivory and salmon are displayed simply in a glass jar on a mantlepiece at Kettle's Yard. The calming restraint of the interior is enhanced by flowers in similarly pared-back palettes. Below: A selection of vibrant dahlias and zinnias in an earthernware jug.

So, in the interests of brevity, what follows is a personal journal of the thoughts and observations that are constantly percolating and evolving in my mind through my work with gardens, plants and flowers.

Throughout, the following terms are used to describe colours. While in everyday language they have all largely become synonymous with one another, from a descriptive point of view, each has a specific meaning that is worth highlighting here:

Hue: A pure colour, the origin of all colours that we see.
Tint: A colour (hue) that has been lightened by the addition of white.
Tone: A colour (hue) that has been either lightened or darkened by the addition of grey.
Shade: A colour (hue) that has been darkened by the addition of black.

I am a gardener who is as thrilled with flowers tumbling from jugs and vases when cut for the house as I am with their performance in the beds and borders of the garden. To me, the two realms coexist to create an unfettered boundary between the inside and the outside, and it is for this reason that the two concepts of growing and arranging are used interchangeably throughout this book. The primary intention is to explore the joy and fantasy of flower colour regardless of which medium

– the garden or the vase – they may appear in, and the hope is that, in doing so, readers might unlock a new way of thinking about the subject.

Instead of viewing flower colour as a one-dimensional decorative element, can it contribute to a much wider sensory experience? Where before a red flower may simply have been thought of as an attractive, but unsophisticated, flash of vermillion, considering instead its function as a building block for creating something more engaging begins to unlock its true power. It is about viewing flower colour as part of an equation. On its own it is one thing, but added to, subtracted from or multiplied, it equals something more profound: an atmosphere.

Combining Flower Colour

'The only principle behind the harmony of colour is one in which the human soul is moved in a deliberate and purposeful way.'

Wassily Kandinsky, *Concerning the Spiritual in Art*, 1911

The Colour Wheel

For all artists – by which I certainly include the gardener and the flower arranger – there is an element of science underpinning the creativity behind colour selection: the colour wheel. First developed by Isaac Newton in the 18th century as a means of illustrating the spectrum of white light, today this wheel is the artist's starting point, providing a grounding in the basics of successfully combining colour. The wheel is underpinned by a complex field of physics, but it is not necessary to become consumed by trying to understand its history and technical applications in order to appreciate its basic teachings. I would argue that every gardener and flower arranger interested in the relationships that colours can create in their work should have at least a passing knowledge of the wheel's core principles, but, as with so many theories, its conventions, once understood, are there to be broken.

The colour wheel is restricted to the display of overarching hues, the purest forms of colours; where we see red, for example, we do not see merlot, cardinal, cherry or ruby. In this way, it is important to recognize that its usefulness is as a broad reference to the relationships created by colour combinations, and that underneath each hue lies a family of colour to which these principles also apply. For instance, what it tells us about blue also concerns blue's long list of subsidiaries: the aquamarines, the sapphires, the ceruleans. This is particularly pertinent to the gardener and the arranger as flower colour rarely, if ever, comes in the form of an unnuanced hue.

A basic colour wheel illustrates the hierarchy of colour in three layers: primaries, secondaries and tertiaries. Although the colours it presents are created in layers of mixing, each is given equal prominence, so that instead of a scale, a continuum is achieved.

Opposite: A simple colour wheel showing the primary, secondary and tertiary hues.

The Primary Triad

The primary triad links the three hues red, yellow and blue. These are the purest of all colours and they form the basis of everything else that surrounds them (red, yellow and blue can be mixed to create any other colour). In their raw forms, these colours carry an inherent confidence and authority, standing out as solid and easy to understand. But what makes the primaries so useful in areas of graphic design – where messages need to be conveyed quickly and succinctly – often makes them unpopular, sometimes unfairly in my opinion, with gardeners and flower arrangers looking for more nuance and intrigue in their choices.

No flower could ever truly be described as primary red, yellow or blue in their purest form. All colours produced by the garden are, to a greater or lesser extent, abstracted in some way, but there are some across the year, highlighted below, that I think come closest:

Primary red
Anemone coronaria 'Hollandia', *Monarda* 'Cambridge Scarlet' (above), *Papaver* Red Rumble

Primary blue
Agapanthus Brilliant Blue, *Hyacinthus orientalis* 'Delft Blue' (above), *Phacelia campanularia*

Primary yellow
Achillea filipendulina 'Cloth of Gold', *Calendula officinalis* 'Calexis Yellow', *Primula veris* (above)

The Secondary Triad

The secondary triad – orange, green and violet – is the result of mixing two primaries. Red and yellow combine to create orange; yellow and blue produce green; and red and blue gives us violet. Although these three hues might feel less decisive than the primaries used to make them, they seem somehow to carry greater complexity, and, with that, they begin to move the eye towards a palette that many would consider more sophisticated.

There is a curious mystery to the secondaries. The strange alchemy of mixing two colours to produce another means that there is always uncertainty about how we, the observer, should respond to them. When encountering orange, for example, do we feel a sense of warmth and contentment – recalling memories of pleasant sunshine on a perfect summer's day – or do we feel threatened by its associations with fire and burning? In the end, the context within which the colour is being used generally makes the answer rather simple, but this initial ambiguity demonstrates the fascinating capacity of colour mixing to create nuance. It is here, in its enigmatic unpredictability, that the powerful emotional impact of colour begins to present itself.

As with the primaries, it would be difficult to suggest that any flower is pure orange, green or violet. However, there are those that I look to as best encapsulating their spirit throughout the year:

Orange
Calendula officinalis 'Indian Prince', *Crocosmia* × *crocosmiiflora* 'Carmin Brillant' (above), *Tithonia rotundifolia* 'Torch'

Green
Dipsacus fullonum (above), *Hosta* 'Devon Green' (foliage only), *Moluccella laevis*

Violet
Allium hollandicum 'Purple Sensation' (above), *Geranium* 'Ann Folkard', *Iris reticulata* 'J.S. Dijt'

COMBINING FLOWER COLOUR

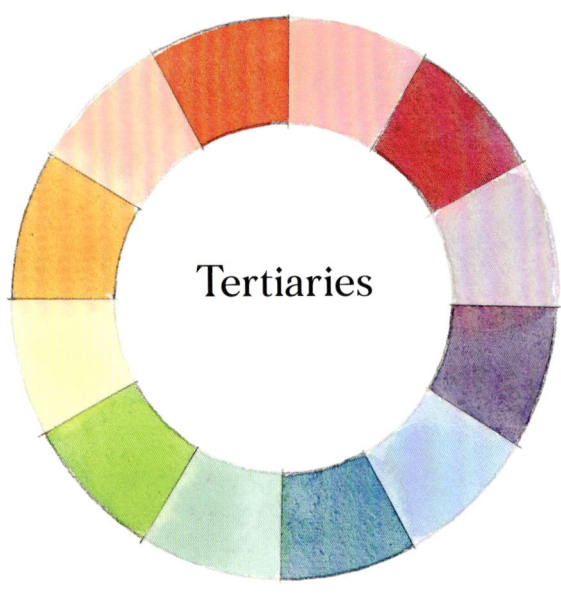

Tertiaries dive even further into colour subtlety. These are colours formed when a primary is mixed with a secondary. Amber, for example, is the result of primary yellow and secondary orange, while chartreuse is created from primary yellow and secondary green. Continuing around the colour wheel, vermillion, teal, indigo and magenta are also added.

These colours show a slight trepidation, as though they're not entirely sure of themselves. To me, they display a distance and depth that reflects their blended provenance, a certain aloofness which is absent from the primaries and less pronounced in the secondaries. Their subserviency affords them a softer and more sympathetic quality that, in the form of flowers, often creates highly desirable and sophisticated hues across the garden and in the vase.

When compared to primaries and secondaries, tertiaries are perhaps easier to attribute to flowers due to their more nuanced pedigree. However, this also leaves them more susceptible to debate – one gardener's violet is another's magenta. My own interpretation of tertiary colour is just one of many:

Opposite: *Cosmos bipinnatus* 'Sensation Radiance' in a jug at the home of Isabel and Julian Bannerman in Somerset. This cosmos is always, to my mind, a good example of tertiary magenta.

Amber
Crocus olivieri subsp. *balansae* 'Orange Monarch', *Narcissus* 'Eaton Song' (above left), *Rosa* Lady of Shalott ('Ausnyson')

Chartreuse
Alchemilla mollis (above centre), *Angelica archangelica*, *Echinacea purpurea* 'Green Jewel'

Vermillion
Crocosmia 'Hellfire', *Geum* 'Mrs J. Bradshaw', *Tulipa* 'Avignon'

Teal
Echinops bannaticus 'Taplow Blue'

Indigo
Delphinium 'Amadeus', *Iris* 'Benton Judith', *Lathyrus odoratus* 'Just Jenny'

Magenta
Digitalis purpurea (above right), *Hyacinthus orientalis* 'Pink Pearl', *Silene coronaria*

Complementary

The primary, secondary and tertiary hues combine to complete the wheel. As artists, we invariably select colours from the wheel in the hope that combining them will be aesthetically harmonious. To achieve this, we can use the wheel very simply to identify the foundations of attractive and melodic palettes.

The most enduring route to balance comes from complementary colours, which sit opposite one another on the wheel. These colours contrast in a way that pulls each one into sharp focus without either appearing to dominate. It is why red flowers – like *Monarda* 'Cambridge Scarlet' – always look so striking against the green of their foliage, and why it is common to find the yellows of daffodils mixed with the blues and violets of grape hyacinths (*Muscari*) and *Scilla luciliae* (formerly *Chionodoxa luciliae*) in spring.

Green plays an interesting role with flower colour. This colour is so inescapable in the garden and the vase that when constructing palettes in a complementary manner, it is either treated as a neutral or used as a colour in its own right. For the latter, the wheel shows us that its complementary colours are red and pink. It could be, for example, that in early summer the chartreuse of lady's mantle (*Alchemilla mollis*) is mixed through the powdery pastel of *Geranium* × *oxonianum* 'Wargrave Pink' or that in spring the acid-green *Euphorbia amygdaloides* var. *robbiae* is paired with the vibrant ruby of *Tulipa* 'Couleur Cardinal'. There are countless more examples, all equally thrilling. However, more often than not, the gardener and flower arranger have a passive relationship with green, using it as a canvas that quietly fades into the background. In this way, it is important to recognize that there can never truly be a pure complementary composition of two hues; even the most tried-and-tested of complementary pairings will, in a floral context, be muddied to some degree by green's presence. For the gardener and arranger, all colour decisions must be seen through a verdant lens.

I rarely think in just two colours. Often, when designing a planting scheme or arranging cut flowers, my mind is too full of ideas to limit myself in this way. That said, it is important to understand the principle behind how pairs draw the best out of each other. A complementary mix is a starting point for me, from which a wider mood can be suggested. So, where I might begin by cutting a bucketful of buttery yellow roses to display inside, I am not usually focused on the fact that blooms in a silky violet would create the optimum aesthetic complement. Instead, I think more broadly about the general atmosphere I'm looking to achieve, which, in the end, may incorporate a complementary element.

Left: A complementary composition of red and green with *Tagetes patula* 'Burning Embers', a French marigold cultivar, and rosehips set against a pistachio wall. Below: *Alchemilla mollis* growing through swathes of pink hardy geraniums creates a moment of complementary interest in the garden. Overleaf: A display of analogous pinks, purples and blues, including *Rosa* Bonica ('Meidomonac'), *Centaurea cyanus* 'Blue Diadem' and 'Classic Fantastic', and *Lathyrus odoratus* 'Bristol' and 'Noel Sutton'.

Examples of seasonal complementary pairings:

Spring
- *Tulipa* 'Negrita' (mid-purple) & *T.* 'Elegant Lady' (butter-yellow)
- *Narcissus* 'Jetfire' (amber) & *Muscari armeniacum* 'Valerie Finnis' (sky-blue)
- *Iris germanica* 'Benton Judith' (indigo) & *I. g.* 'Benton Olive' (mid-yellow)

Summer
- *Alchemilla mollis* (chartreuse) & *Penstemon* 'Andenken an Friedrich Hahn' (magenta)
- *Allium hollandicum* 'Purple Sensation' (mid-purple) & *Digitalis grandiflora* (lemon-yellow)
- *Nigella damascena* 'Miss Jekyll' (sky-blue) & *Papaver rupifragum* 'Orange Feathers' (mid-orange)

Autumn
- *Cosmos bipinnatus* 'Xanthos' (butter-yellow) & *Scabiosa atropurpurea* 'Black Knight' (dark purple)
- *Dahlia* 'David Howard' (apricot-orange) & *Salvia uliginosa* (sky-blue)
- *Tagetes patula* 'Burning Embers' (mid-red) & *Echinacea purpurea* 'Green Jewel' (chartreuse)

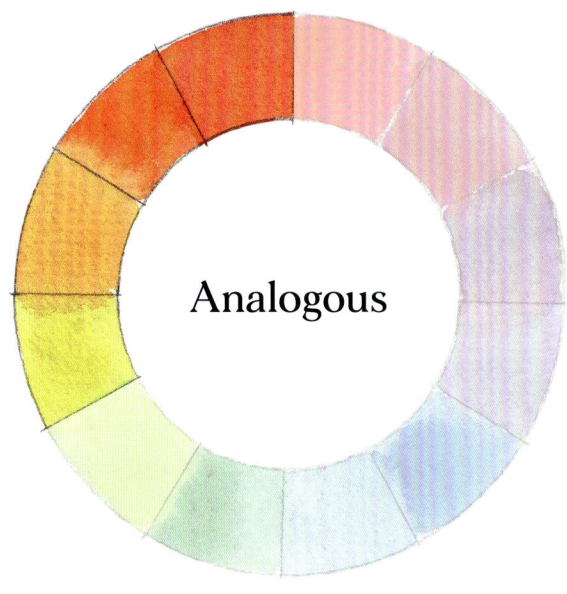

Analogous groups are another avenue to harmonious palettes. These are colours that sit next to each other on the wheel – examples could be red, orange and yellow, or green, blue and violet. As neighbours, they share the same sentiment, and, when building a scheme, they have the effect of appearing like a good-natured extended family.

Unlike pairs of complementary colours, I am always more likely to be thinking of an analogous group. This is the opportunity to build a story with flower colour, to explore moods with greater depth. It is the romance of a border in early summer as the electric pinks of *Lychnis coronaria* drift through the silky apricots of *Rosa* Boscobel ('Auscousin') and the dusty violets of *Nepeta racemosa* 'Walker's Low'. It is garden flowers in blues and greens brought into the house to provide a moment of calm.

In very basic terms, there are three analogous moods arising from the wheel that most inform how I view the assembly of flower colour:

Romantic: pinks, purples and softer reds
Energetic: reds, yellows and oranges
Reflective: greens, blues and (although not strictly a colour on the wheel) whites

Exploring the atmospheres that these colour families create underpins much of how I work with plants and flowers. However, as with the principle of complementary pairings, it is only ever really a starting point. The fun, for me, is always in their subtle undoing: what happens when two mood groups collide? Blues are analogous to pinks and purples, but does blue add to or detract from the romance of pink and purple? Where greens and blues are reflective and soothing, what impact does the addition of yellow have on the overall mood? The answers to these questions are, of course, entirely subjective, and that is precisely what makes their investigation so thrillingly diverse from one flower lover to the next.

Examples of analogous groups:

Spring
• *Iris germanica* 'Benton Nigel' (indigo), *I. g.* 'Ciel et Mer' (mid-blue and ivory) & *I. g.* 'Sapphire Hills' (powder blue)
• *Narcissus* 'Eaton Song' (amber), *N.* 'Eclat' (mid-orange and ivory) & *N.* 'Red Devon' (gold and amber)
• *Tulipa* 'Albert Heijn' (candy pink), *T.* 'Blushing Lady' (peach-pink) & *T.* 'Queen of Night' (dark purple)

Summer
• *Delphinium* 'Amadeus' (indigo), *Euphorbia amygdaloides* var. *robbiae* (chartreuse) & *Geranium* Rozanne (blue-mauve)
• *Rosa* 'Constance Spry' (baby pink), *R.* Young Lycidas ('Ausvibrant') (magenta) & *R.* Munstead Wood ('Ausbernard') (merlot)

Autumn
• *Dahlia* 'Blitzer' (apricot-orange), *D.* 'Bishop of York' (amber) & *D.* 'Graceland' (orange)
• *Dahlia* 'Feline Yvonne' (powder pink), *D.* 'Hillcrest Candy' (powder pink) & *D.* Happy Single Juliet (lilac)

COMBINING FLOWER COLOUR

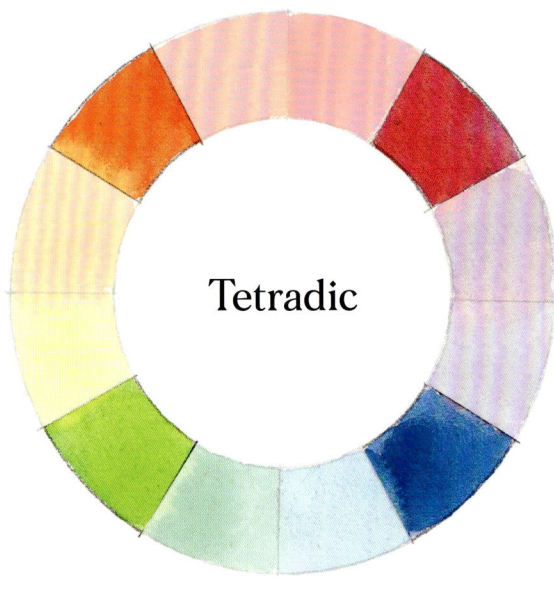

Tetradic

While there is a reliability in complementary pairs and analogous groups, there also comes a certain predictability. Too much harmony risks the eye becoming bored, which is why often the most successful visual communication introduces a challenge to the viewer by using palettes that go beyond the instinctive.

A tetradic colour combination is an interesting way of maintaining some sense of harmony while introducing an element of friction. Overlaying a rectangle onto the wheel selects four colours, of which there are two sets of complementary pairs. While separately each pair provides a sense of cohesion, when the eye cross-pollinates them, a moment of compelling discord arises.

In a vase, the sunset-orange of *Geum* 'Totally Tangerine' mixed with the plum of the poppy *Papaver somniferum* 'Lauren's Grape', the cerulean of cornflowers (*Centaurea cyanus*) and the chartreuse of lady's mantle (*Alchemilla mollis*) would combine to present a tetradic display. Here, the geum and the cornflowers are complementary, but the geum and the *Alchemilla mollis* are a more surprising match. As the eye travels around the arrangement, it is caught in a dilemma: focus on that which is most visually pleasing or attempt to resolve the conflict created between the more unpredictable colour partnerships? The result is usually a marriage of the two, the eye bouncing between the safe and the insecure.

These schemes begin to suggest a mood before quickly pulling back and deciding on another. The palette is indecisive, and it is this oscillation that has the potential to create thrilling and novel combinations of colour in the garden and in the vase.

Opposite: A tetradic display of late summer flowers. The burned oranges of *Rudbeckia hirta* 'Autumn Colours' and *Crocosmia × crocosmiiflora* 'Emily Mckenzie' complement the dusty blues of *Aster × frikartii* 'Mönch', while the mid-green foliage of the rudbeckia complements the magenta of *Dahlia* 'Franz Kafka'.

Examples of seasonal tetradic pairings:

Spring
Tulipa 'Albert Heijn' (candy pink) & *T.* 'Green Spirit' (mid-green–ivory) with *T.* 'Cairo' (burned orange) & *T.* 'Bleu Aimable' (blue-mauve)

Summer
Alchemilla mollis (chartreuse) & *Rosa* Boscobel ('Auscousin') (candy pink) with *Geranium* Rozanne (blue-mauve) & *Geum* 'Totally Tangerine' (tangerine)

Autumn
Cosmos bipinnatus 'Casanova Pink' (powder pink) & *Zinnia elegans* 'Envy' (chartreuse) with *Scabiosa* Kudo Blue (powder blue) & *Tithonia rotundifolia* 'Torch' (mid-orange)

Liberation

The colour wheel attempts to offer a sense of order, but what happens when these conventions are ignored, and the freedom of creative self-expression is given permission to take precedence over science?

Thinking about flower colour without prejudice unlocks a new world of atmosphere. What might at first feel riotous and unruly may actually excite and stimulate; where colours feel incongruous and clashing, their naivety may, in fact, evoke a sense of romance. I am always of the opinion that the use of colour wheel theory should be light when creating personal flower displays: allow it to gently inform rather than dictate; respect its science but resolve to make up your own mind based on experimentation.

It is also important to let go of preconceived ideas about what constitutes horticultural good taste if the aim is to explore flower colour with utmost liberation. As with anything creative in life, flowers are the subject of changing trends, and their colours constantly fall in and out of favour according to the fickle whims of fashion. The gardener may get immense joy from the brightest, egg-yolk-yellow daffodils in spring, but a prevailing trend for tastemakers, commentators and garden institutions to use flowers in more subtle tones may induce a hesitation to plant them. I've lost count of the number of times that I have heard the same thing said about certain colours – a hatred of yellow, an aversion to orange, difficulty with blue – and almost always these opinions are following some current trend or other.

As people we have a natural desire to fit in (we are social animals after all), but in the areas of our lives where we have the most freedom to express ourselves – the way we dress, the way we decorate our homes, what our garden looks like – we all too often allow that need for acceptance to interfere with what actually makes us happy. To my mind, plants and flowers are used most successfully when the gardener or flower arranger places their full focus on how they hope to feel and not, as is too often the case, on whether what they are creating is right.

Opposite: A display of zinnias in a riotous and unpretentious mix of saturated hues. Often the most endearing and captivating of floral displays are those that are not laboured over with a desire to achieve perfect colour harmony.

The Effect of White

White, in terms of the colour wheel, is not a colour; it is, in fact, the reflection of all light wavelengths. However, in anything concerning the arts, it is impossible to ignore the influence that white has when thought of and used in the same way as any other hue. Indeed, white flowers are incredibly common across the plant kingdom and to overlook them would be to severely curtail a planting scheme or cut flower display.

When combined with one other colour, white has the effect of drawing the eye towards its accompaniment; it recedes and pushes its partner forward, which is effective when the intention is to make a colour statement. It could be the amber glow of *Narcissus* 'Red Devon' emerging through ivory drifts of *N.* 'Polar Ice', or perhaps the blazing fireworks of *Monarda* 'Cambridge Scarlet' erupting among pearly clouds of Baltic parsley (*Cenolophium denudatum*). Here, the yellow narcissus and the red monarda appear more intense due to the neutral backdrop provided by white. Quite simply, the eye is relieved of distraction.

But white is an enigma. Where it highlights, it can also subdue, and soft, pastel flower colour can quickly become overwhelmed by its presence. In a vase, the delicate peach of *Rosa* Emily Brontë ('Ausearnshaw') is completely lost when paired with the chalky white of *R.* Desdemona ('Auskindling'). The same effect is seen when the pale and buttery yellow of *Cosmos bipinnatus* 'Xanthos' is obscured by the intensity of *C. bipinnatus* 'Sonata White', and when *Lathyrus odoratus* 'Queen of Hearts' (an ivory sweet pea tinged with pink) completely washes away the powdery blue in *L.* × *hammettii* 'Turquoise Lagoon'. White here has an overexposure effect; it floods the eye with achromic neutrality to the point that subtle deviations in tone are difficult to identify.

White as part of a wider colour palette either tempers or heightens a mood. With hot pinks and purples in a romantic scheme, white can have a grounding effect, pulling back a display before it becomes too saccharine. It has a similar influence in an energetic grouping of reds, oranges and yellows; here, white introduces a moment of restraint, affording the eye space to fully digest the scene. Yet, in a reflective setting of blues and greens, the application of white only serves to intensify a sense of serenity and restoration; it plays into the theme instead of moderating it.

There is a risk with white that its impact in the garden or in a cut flower display is underestimated. White is a powerful ingredient in any palette, one that perhaps more than any other has the power to enhance, weaken or distort nearby colours.

Left: The ivory clouds of the umbellifer *Cenolophium denudatum* push the flaming flower heads of *Monarda* 'Cambridge Scarlet' forward in this planting composition. Opposite: The enduring simplicity of white flowers. In this display, lacy *Ammi majus* is mixed with *Malva trimestris* 'Mont Blanc', Phlox and *Tanacetum parthenium* to create a timeless and incredibly soothing composition.

The Effect of Background

Green, in its ubiquity, becomes a silent partner to any palette in the garden, a verdant canvas that retreats to a kind of neutral. Yet inside, the influence of background colour on displays of cut flowers is more discretionary. In accordance with colour wheel harmony, a blue room is primed for flowers in complementary orange, while a room in red waits for a display of green foliage. However, often the vases we create for the house are spontaneous and there is little desire to have them perfectly in tune with the interior palette. Indeed, these impromptu flowers are always my favourite to display indoors, but sometimes there are occasions when it is fun to be more considered and, in so doing, play with the impact that the surrounding indoor scheme creates.

In these instances, it is the mood that a combination of room colour and flower display evokes that is most thrilling to me. Perhaps it is a white interior where blazing reds, oranges and yellows appear even more energetic, the neutrality of the space receding to draw the eye's full attention towards the display's vivacity. Perhaps it is a densely decorated room with walls in a rich cardinal red with a display of blousy roses in sumptuous pinks to create a whimsical feeling of romance. Either way, the house becomes a stage – a fantasy dreamscape – where interior decoration and garden blooms coalesce to inspire an evocative atmosphere.

It might be that only sections of a room provide a backdrop: a colourful bookshelf, a deep windowsill, a certain picture or work of art on the wall, for example. Different constituent parts of an interior hold a multitude of possibilities for flower displays, and often the most surprising of places produce the most thrilling results.

Opposite: A charming display of *Narcissus* 'Actaea' against a salmon-pink wall at Charleston, in East Sussex, the home of artists Vanessa Bell and Duncan Grant. The imperfection of the wall, with its crumbly and weathered texture, plays against the exacting precision of the daffodil petals.

The Effect of Light

Light has a profound effect on flower colour, and it can dramatically alter the ways in which different tints, tones and shades interact with one another in a scheme. In the gentle light of a mid-summer sunrise, colour across the garden appears distinct and unblemished; there is a melodic quality and hues feel perfectly balanced and proportionate. The plums of *Salvia* and *Nepeta* are total and resolute; the powdery pinks of roses are pure and unspoiled; the brilliance of white ox-eye daisy (*Leucanthemum vulgare*) is unsullied. But this does not last long. As the sun climbs, so too does the harshness with which light hits the planting. Suddenly, flowers are bleached and shadowed; a greater glare develops that washes out nuance and intricacy. Flowers that earlier sat harmoniously with one another now appear disparate and detached.

In this way, flower colour cannot be seen as static. It evolves throughout the day, and where one area of planting shines, another may retreat. In the midday sun, flowers that at other times appear dark and brooding, unveil their hidden depths: *Tulipa* 'Continental' emerges from a black cloak to reveal petals in raspberry-jam red; *Dahlia* 'Sam Hopkins' lifts from a shadowy maroon to a deep crimson; the sweet pea *Lathyrus odoratus* 'Beaujolais' transforms from an inky raisin to a resplendent cranberry. But noon sunshine can also overwhelm: *Astrantia* 'Buckland' loses its delicate frosting of pink, the ruffled apricot petals of *Narcissus* 'Cum Laude' become diluted, the buttery translucence of *Cosmos bipinnatus* 'Xanthos' is overexposed.

In the house, the instability of flower colours in different lights can be leveraged to interesting effect. Placed directly in front of a light source like a window, backlighting a display casts flowers into shadow. This may seem counterintuitive, but where subtlety of colour is lost, a greater sense of the display's overall shape is illuminated, and this can be attractive when the objective is to appreciate decorative form.

Placing bright flowers such as *Dahlia* 'Kelvin Floodlight' or *Tulipa* 'Candela' in shadowy, forgotten corners of the house undoubtedly mutes their vibrancy. Yet such is the strength of their character that they cannot help but still bring a sense of life and vitality to these duller areas. My cottage has many of

these dark and moody alcoves, and it is in those places that I often like to position the most exuberant of displays. Without them, it is easy for me to be dragged into a kind of malaise when spending time in such lustreless areas. However, these displays somehow seem to penetrate the half-light, spreading a feeling of joy within the gloom that radiates through me.

There is something incredibly comforting in the way that golden evening light gently caresses a display of flowers at the end of the day. For example, a jug of yellows and oranges – perhaps daffodils in early spring – appears to melt into more complex ambers and apricots; roses in reds and pinks become haloed with marmalade; greens and blues seem to bounce with greater vigour; whites – like a charming cup of lily of the valley (*Convallaria majalis*) – thaw into bronze and copper. These are fleeting moments that bring untold joy to everyday life, a performance that feels intimate and personal in the quiet sanctuary of home.

Artificial light presents further complexity. Similar to the harshness of midday sun in the garden, it has the effect of increasing contrast and can erode the intricacy of a flower's pigmentation. Depending on the warmth or coolness of the light, it can also alter the overall mood of the display. Where warm light increases a sense of exuberance with flowers in reds and oranges, it can also dampen the romance of pinks and purples. Where cool light lifts the softness of reflective greens and blues, it pulls back the energy of yellows.

Opposite: In bright midday sunshine, *Cosmos atrosanguineus* has glossy petals similar in colour to Beaujolais wine, yet among the shadows of the house, the flowers transform into the colour of dark blackberry jam. Above: A display of sweet peas (*Lathyrus odoratus*) backlit by light from a small window.

Value and Temperature

Every colour has a value – the brightness or darkness with which it appears relative to its surroundings. Lighter values (like a canary yellow or a sky-blue) have the effect of leaping forward in a composition, whereas darker values (like a deep indigo or a rich merlot) have the opposite effect, appearing to recede into the background. In this way, there is a push and pull to colour, a play of vibrancy that intrigues the eye.

When lighter and darker values are combined, a sense of depth and movement is created. Depth has curiosity; it presents the eye with an irresistible challenge, forcing the observer to investigate the scene's layers. Movement introduces urgency, a sense of the scene in flux; the eye is encouraged to consider a journey and is left with a tantalizing question: what happens next?

In a spring display of tulips, it would be the dark values of mysterious almost-blacks like 'Continental', 'Queen of Night' and 'Indeland' together with the deep reds of 'Armani', 'Couleur Cardinal' and 'Lasting Love' that retired to the background. They would appear shadowy and reticent compared to the lighter values of whites, peaches, apricots and yellows (like 'Cash', 'Françoise', 'City of Vancouver' and 'Daydream'), which would rush to command the foreground with exuberance. In between the two extremes, the pinks, salmons and violets (perhaps 'Pretty Princess', 'La Belle Époque' and 'Night Club') would occupy the mid-ground, binding the whole performance together with a unifying mid-value neutrality. Overall, there would be weight and substance, a sense of volume that encouraged the eye to explore the display in three dimensions.

However, in considering depth, value is not the only determinant: the effect of a colour's temperature also has an influence. In simple terms, it is reds, oranges and yellows that lean warm, while blues, greens and purples face towards cool. These hues group themselves neatly in this respect, but the nuance of flower colour often creates a complexity. *Geranium* 'Dilys', for example, would broadly be described as purple (and thus cool), yet it is a colour with a bias towards red and so it becomes warm. Similarly, *Tulipa* 'Candela' is, on the surface, yellow, but a strong green influence tips it into the cool spectrum. So, it is not always a straightforward, useful or entirely objective task to assign temperatures to flowers. But it is beneficial to consider the overall effect they have in a composition: like light values, warm colours push forward and cool colours, mirroring the darks, appear to retreat.

Across all floral arrangements, whether as plants in the garden or as cut flowers in the vase, there are three fields of vision: foreground, mid-ground and background. How each aspect is populated is largely determined by the compositional mix of light and dark values together with warm and cool temperatures. In this way, a consideration of how each interacts allows colour to become more than just a decorative feature; it becomes a structural tool, the building blocks of dynamic floral architecture.

Above: A good illustration of colour value comes from the 'Sensation Mix' of annual cosmos, which produces flowers in an ivory white, a powdery pink and a deep claret. The value of the white flower is significantly brighter than the other two, and it appears to jump forward as a result. Opposite: A display of late summer flowers mixing light, mid and dark values.

Atmosphere

Ultimately, the success of floral colour combinations in the garden and the vase is always for me about the extent to which an atmosphere is created and felt. The wisdom and conventions of the colour wheel are, I suppose, always etched into my mind, but they are echoey suggestions rather than guiding lights. Instead of dictating my work, they lightly inform a certain underlying framework from which I allow myself the freedom to explore. A shot of amber may undo an otherwise perfectly analogous display of cut roses in various pinks if it strikes me as adding to a sense of romance, or swathes of energetic tulips in yellows and oranges may be interrupted here and there by magenta if I think that it heightens the feeling of vitality. It is about tuning into the way I want to feel, understanding the cues that certain colours – and combinations of colour – give to me.

This is a personal endeavour, one that perhaps no two people would approach in the same way. There are no rules or guidelines, no right or wrong – the only limitations are those placed arbitrarily on the imagination.

Opposite: Roses in a playful mix of candied pinks and butter-yellows. This syrupy palette has a way of transporting me to a dreamworld of whimsical romance, the humdrum of the everyday momentarily forgotten. Above: Bright, bold and uncompromising, this riotous mix of dahlias, zinnias and rudbeckias fizzes with an infectious sense of energy.

Atmosphere 1:
Romantic

Twilight in late spring. The first hint of rose perfume as the sky darkens, petals unfurling into dusty pink cushions. Foxgloves (*Digitalis purpurea*) and bearded irises (*Iris germanica*) shooting skyward in mauves and lilacs. The air whispers softly with romance. Something has changed in the garden; suddenly the youthful optimism of early bulbs in electric blues and sunshine-yellows has been replaced by a sophisticated palette of cerises, corals and magentas. As darkness approaches, the whole landscape settles into a contented stillness. Birds with full bellies and the promise of a productive tomorrow retreat to their roosts, while over in the woodland, the night belongs to secretive nymphs and mischievous sprites.

Unlocking a sense of romance drives almost everything I do in the garden; it is an endless quest in search of a maddeningly abstract feeling. Perfect imperfection, unbridled abundance mixed with a casual nonchalance. It is self-seeded Mexican fleabane (*Erigeron karvinskianus*) popping up in clouds between cracks in paving, cow parsley (*Anthriscus sylvestris*) and valerian drifting effortlessly under burgeoning canopies of beech (*Fagus sylvatica*); there is a deference to the garden's unpredictability. Where our lives have become ordered and routine, an escape is found in nature's wonderful chaos.

Opposite: Romantic scrapbook. A selection of the pinks and purples that come together to fill my head with fanciful daydreams of long, sun-soaked days lost in the haze of summer abundance.

A World of Whimsical Imperfection

I am often consumed by the question of what exactly is meant when a garden or flower display is considered romantic. On the surface, I can point to the fact that, for me, colour is certainly an important factor, but what are the other, perhaps less tangible, details with which a palette must combine to inspire this abstract sensibility? Is colour alone ever enough?

In search of answers, I suppose in many ways it is about unlocking the magic in every moment, finding a sense of beauty when only the mundane seems present. A weekday supper elevated by impossibly full jugs of dahlias, forgotten corners of the house awoken by leggy pelargoniums, a handful of cut tulips given to a friend, an hour or two dozing by the river on a late spring afternoon with a handful of wildflowers.

The garden as romantic is a well-established concept, and the idea that within it we might lose ourselves to some fantastically whimsical alternate reality is a theme that has recurred in countless ways throughout art and literature. From the sylvan enchantment of Shakespeare's *A Midsummer Night's Dream* to the idealized and sentimental paintings of John Constable, artists have long indulged in nature's inherent sense of otherness to create fantasy dreamworlds of seduction and intrigue. But, again, I ask myself: what are these works capturing?

Is it that we are chasing a lost arcadia? Every new generation of artists and artist-gardeners looks to the generations of the past as representative of some perfect idyll, yearning for a time more sensitive and enlightened than their own. I, for one, cannot help but look back through the 20th century at artist-gardeners such as Cedric Morris, Cecil Beaton, Vanessa Bell and Gertrude Jekyll as having enjoyed a more fulfilling and creatively stimulating relationship with the garden, a sense that theirs was a time less marred and interrupted by all the messy complications of modern-day life. While there is undoubtedly a risk of oversimplifying the past and falsely assuming that a less digital world equalled a greater kind of freedom and innocence, it is this constant pursuit of a time less tethered to machines and more sensitive to the land that I think begins to form the root of romanticism in my mind.

On a more practical level, I suppose when I interrogate the gardens and displays of cut flowers that I would consider to be romantic, each one always has one concrete thing in common: a sense of imperfection. With imperfection comes a unique kind of attractiveness; it is the allure of personality, the feeling of individualism and character. We are charmed by a garden or flower display's flaws because there is no assertion of superiority; it is not looking to impress in a way that is haughty or arrogant. It does not try to overawe with excellence. By being open and conscious of its shortcomings, a garden or flower display pulls us in – it invites investigation – and this honesty is, I think, endlessly romantic.

Driving through the country lanes of Somerset near to where I live, there are countless little cottages where the gardens shine with whimsical imperfection. Places where in spring wild garlic or ramsons (*Allium ursinum*) and forget-me-nots (*Myosotis sylvatica*) creep ever more out of control, while in summer hollyhocks (*Alcea rosea*) sprawl from cracks in stone walls. These are not the glorified plots we see in magazines or lauded on social media; these are gardens of quiet and private romance. This sense of having created your own intimate dreamworld – somewhere teeming with the plants and flowers that bring personal joy – is something that is feverishly evocative to me. I am fascinated by the idea of cocooning myself within the garden, creating a place that somehow feels detached

Previous pages, from left to right: Candy floss-pink *Rosa* Boscobel ('Auscousin') mixed with salmon-pink *R*. 'Albertine' and golden 'Emily Gray' at the window of my cottage; *Iris orientalis*, roses and pink hardy geraniums in the cottage garden in high summer; a playful mix of bearded iris (*Iris germanica*) and foxgloves (*Digitalis purpurea*) in a jug.

from the dogma of life that surrounds it. It is as though entering my garden is to enter the chaotic and fanciful chambers of my imagination. Perfection is not sought because this place belongs solely to me; it remains as flawed and idiosyncratic as I am myself.

However, privacy does not equal isolation. In fact, to my mind, a significant characteristic of romanticism is the sharing of the garden with friends. Summer suppers that stretch late into the evening; spring lunches that turn into whole afternoons; the simple pleasure of walking through the garden with a loved one. Romanticism is surely a combined creative energy: the exchange of ideas, a spirited but convivial debate.

Flowers are a central feature for the romantic gardener. Could we ever have too many? In spring, I want bulbs to explode in bountiful drifts; in summer, I want roses of all kinds to erupt in a kind of farcical display of abundance; in autumn, I want annuals to completely take over every inch of remaining space. Above all else, their colours are what I crave. It is the coyness of pinks, the ambiguity of purples; pastels layered upon the saturated, softness embracing strength. For me, colour is the binding force of romanticism, the ingredient that lifts a floral display from the attractive to the atmospheric, and it is always with the suggestion of a powdery coral, a dusty mauve or a candied cerise that every romantic whim of my imagination begins.

*

It is sometimes easier to appreciate an atmosphere when it comes from somewhere less immediately familiar than your own space. It is the sense of becoming lost in someone else's fantasy, travelling the contours of a foreign imagination. Exploring the dreamworlds of others is something I find forever fascinating and deeply inspiring. It helps me to better understand my own creative impulses, giving me space to scrutinize the triggers that ignite excitement inside me.

The people and places that feature over the following pages have all cultivated their own personal sense of romance, and it is an appreciation of the decorative potential of flowers – particularly pertaining to the colour that they bring to both the garden and the vase – that unites each.

Opposite left: A romantic summer display of roses, foxgloves, bearded iris and love-in-a-mist (*Nigella damascena*). Opposite right: A handful of cut roses in a little cup, including candy floss-pink *R*. Boscobel ('Auscousin'), *R*. Blue Moon ('Tannacht') and apricot-orange 'Just Joey'. Above: The cottage garden blooming in mid-summer – an enchanting realm, a place of enveloping romance. Overleaf: Powdery pink *Rosa* 'Constance Spry' on a shelf alongside buttery *R*. Roald Dahl ('Ausowlish').

ATMOSPHERE 1: ROMANTIC

A Headlong Romance with Roses
Sam McKnight, MBE

COLOUR PROFILE:
Soft pastels, sugary mauves and powdered pinks.
A gentle blanket of candied lilacs, apricots and blush salmon.

In West London, as life spins by in a whirlwind of drama and machines, one of the most romantic urban gardens I can think of sits in glorious incongruity in the noisy and concreted city that surrounds it. This home belongs to celebrated hairstylist Sam McKnight MBE, who is someone, he tells me, that discovered the joy of gardening later in life. Originally designed by Jo Thompson in 2014, this is a place of pure abandon, a fantasy that in summer reaches a floriferous climax with its boundless display of roses.

Roses dominate the garden in a way that feels wonderfully enveloping and reassuring. A terrace is shrouded in an ivory blanket of *Rosa* 'Rambling Rector'; a decorative arch is swathed in the mid-pink fantasy of the Seven Sisters' rose (*Rosa multiflora* 'Grevillei'); and the blooms of 'Guinée' scale the front façade of the house in a sumptuous claret. Countless more rose varieties sprawl from borders and climb through trellises to create an extraordinary level of abundance that completely bewitches the senses. That iconic rose scent – spicy, fruity, honeyed – hangs heavy in the air and, thrillingly, seems to linger long in the mind for some time after leaving.

Opposite: Sam McKnight's garden in high summer. Shrouding an archway in a blousy cloud of hypnotic pink, the Seven Sisters' rose (*Rosa multiflora* 'Grevillei') marks the start of a hypnotic and highly romantic colour journey.

Perennials provide an underplanting. In shadier corners this takes the form of ferns, Solomon's seal (*Polygonatum × hybridum*) and geraniums, whereas sunnier sites are home to geums, salvias and crocosmias. It is a subtle tapestry that bounces a sub-layer of colour and texture through the scheme without attempting to compete with the flamboyant procession of roses overhead. Although the bones of Jo Thompson's original plan remain, the planting is a continuous evolution, with Sam routinely editing and adding to the composition. The rose remains his particular weakness, the seemingly impossible task of finding more space for a new variety is a constant challenge.

The haphazard (and often downright disorderly) way in which roses flower means that this garden always retains an air of informality. Any sense of rigidity, straight lines or ninety-degree angles is tempered by a cascade of ruffled petals falling one on top of the other. Flowers soften every edge, so that transitions between hard and soft landscaping are gentle and blurred, the eye seeming to take pleasure in tracing the garden's fluid contours. There are moments when you would be forgiven for believing this garden sat nestled in a rural valley and not, as the occasional passing tube train reminds you, in the middle of London's Zone Two. This play between city and country, this *rus in urbe*, is precisely what makes the garden so utterly romantic to me. It is the cross-pollination of two realms, the union of two competing ideas. It evokes a surreal sense of abandoning reality in favour of something altogether more magical.

Sam is under no doubt that his biggest joy is the colour these roses bring to the summer garden. Sometimes subtle, sometimes brash; this is a place where colour is revered not only for its ornamental quality, but also its therapeutic properties. As he explains:

'I have come more and more to realize and appreciate just how much colour positively affects my psyche. I am certain that just being around [it] brings a small dopamine hit…Give me a home where the [full colour of] hardy annuals roam and I am the happiest guy in town.'

In an age when our towns and cities are becoming more and more devoid of wildlife and natural spaces, there is something incredibly reassuring about Sam's garden. There is a sense of fightback here – a feeling of resilience – and, to me, this challenge is in itself romantic. It is the struggle to be heard, the taking on of a seemingly unstoppable force. If a garden such as this, so bountiful in its joyful summer colour, could not persuade the most apathetic urban dweller to reconsider their open space, it is hard to think what else ever could.

Previous pages, clockwise from left: The Seven Sisters' rose (*Rosa multiflora* 'Grevillei'); in spring, silky *Tulipa* 'La Belle Époque' emerges through alpine forget-me-nots (*Myosotis alpestris*); ivory clouds of *Rosa* 'Rambling Rector'; the curving lawn at the centre of the design; shrub roses collide with climbers, creating layers of texture. Opposite: In spring, drifts of *Tulipa* 'Ballade' bring waves of concentrated hot pink ahead of the rose spectacle.

A French Kiss
Marin Montagut

COLOUR PROFILE:
*Dusty pinks, raspberry jam and coral.
A fairy tale of syrupy plums, lavender and flushed porcelain.*

Three hundred miles south of Sam McKnight, in the valley of Iton in eastern Normandy, lies a place equally as romantic but altogether more bucolic. Set within fields of wildflowers, the country cottage of designer Marin Montagut and his husband, actor Alexis Gilot, is a place where the whims of imagination are not only indulged but actively encouraged.

Like all the best cottages, Marin's home appears to rise effortlessly from the landscape. It is as though over time the fields gently parted and, quite naturally, in their place grew stone walls cloaked in climbing vines, a patinaed slate roof and shutters painted in plum. When Marin was searching for a cottage to rent outside Paris in 2010, a friend suggested this place, and, upon visiting, it was love at first sight: 'I immediately knew this is where I wanted to settle…it looked like such a joyful house.'

The interior has a casual disregard for order. Artefacts and curiosities line the walls; pottery and glassware sit stacked on antique dressers; multicoloured fabrics lie strewn across floors, sofas and chairs. The whole place feels textured and complex, the embodiment of the couple's varied creative interests. But through the melee of different objects that fight for space in this compact cottage, there remains one constant: flowers.

Opposite: Powdery pastel-pink tulips brought from a friend's garden in Paris to Marin's home in Normandy. A cottage radiating with romance, these delicately coloured tulips heighten the feeling of having momentarily escaped from the routine of everyday life.

Displays of garden blooms feel so at home here, seeming to blend effortlessly into the informality of the interior. They enhance a sense of wild abandon, a feeling of unfettered romance. There are handfuls of tulips escaping from jugs next to old postcards, antique candlesticks and small glass cups; wildflowers picked from the surrounding fields and placed on bookcases that are thronged with antique tomes; a garden table dressed for supper with a few simple cups of roses.

The garden has a delightful simplicity; for the most part it remains long grass with a mowed path, giving access to a seating area under a mature beech. A small mixed border edges the front of the cottage, which, in spring, becomes a pastel wave of tulips in dusky pinks and powdery purples (the attractive *T.* 'Groenland', in the Viridiflora Group, is a notable example). Bearded iris (*Iris germanica*), which come later, have formed large colonies and predate Marin's time at the house.

What is so enchanting about this place is that nothing ever feels forced. There is no sense of pretence or conceit; objects and flowers have a personal connection to Marin and Alexis, and they land wherever they so wish within the house. Anything remotely contrived would feel jarring and completely at odds with the crudeness of the landscape that forms the borrowed backdrop to their life there. A landscape that so often informs Marin's work, as he told me while painting in the calm of his studio: 'Mainly, I come here to find inspiration.'

Colours throughout the house are rusticated and have a feeling of age. A bedroom painted in a stony pink, the sitting room an earthy yellow. While bright, these colours appear sensitive to the landscape. They do not dominate or attempt to overshadow the circus of textures that arise from soft furnishings, furniture, personal objects and flowers from the garden. Instead, they provide a playful, yet robust canvas upon which everything else hangs.

Previous pages, from left to right: An informal jug of tulips waiting to be brought indoors; the simplest of vessels are used to display tulips across the cottage. Opposite: Normandy scrapbook – the dreamworld of Marin's cottage. Overleaf: A table in the garden prepared for lunch. This is a place where the outdoor and indoor realms seem to flow organically into one another.

The Romance of the Artist-Gardener
Charleston, East Sussex

COLOUR PROFILE:
*Crumbly salmons, earthy merlots and gritty terracotta.
A treasure box of whimsical pastels.*

Charleston has a history that has long fascinated those interested in the cultural zeitgeist of the early 20th century. The East Sussex home of artist-gardeners Vanessa Bell, her lover Duncan Grant, and his partner David Garnett, is a house and garden that became much more than a home: it became the subject of art and, thrillingly, became the art itself. Its rooms and garden appear in countless works by Bell and Grant – there was clearly an interest in capturing the beauty of domestic simplicity – but it is perhaps the way in which its walls, furniture, fixtures and fittings were themselves treated like canvases for which the house is best known.

This is a place that positively froths with romance. A house not only of artistic freedom, but of sexual liberation too: a destination for the most progressive thinkers of the day. But given that the last occupant of Charleston died some thirty years ago, its romance is rooted in the past and locked in the intrigue of the lives that went before.

Opposite: Duncan Grant's dressing room at Charleston. A door painted by Vanessa Bell in 1918 leads to a bookcase topped with silhouettes depicting members of the Grant family. At the centre, an antique ceramic tankard displays a large handful of fried-egg daffodils – *Narcissus* 'Pink Charm'. Layers of colour from decorative objects, art and fabrics combine to produce a place of tantalizing romance.

Above: Charleston in unbroken spring sunshine. Playful urns sit on top of gateposts, which were designed by Vanessa Bell's son, artist Quentin Bell. Opposite: *Narcissus* 'Cragford' displayed in the kitchen. Ornamental objects, fabrics and painted ceramics create a rich, idiosyncratic texture that lends itself perfectly to informally arranged cut flowers.

Garden flowers and their display throughout the interior was a recurring motif in Bell's work. In *View into a Garden* a jug of roses sits on a stool by the back door of her studio; in *The Dining Room Window* a pot of red tulips sits next to a window that looks out onto the lake at the front of the property; in *Charleston Drawing Room* a vase of sweet peas sits on the windowsill alongside roses on the mantlepiece above the fireplace. Countless other examples exist, each sharing a common theme of effortless simplicity. There are no extravagant and overworked floral arrangements; there is no sense of any great thought having gone into the displays. Instead, we are presented with unfussy flowers that add decoration to the rooms on account of simply being there.

There was an intrinsic relationship between the outdoors and the indoors at Charleston, and it seems the garden was planted as much for its decorative potential inside as for the ornamental appeal of beds and borders. In a 1936 letter to her son, Julian, Bell wrote of her excitement at finally having created a bountiful rose garden, but, tellingly, her enthusiasm was as much about the opportunity she now had to display the blooms across the house as it was for their performance in the garden: 'At last I actually have a rose garden – enough roses to pick a bowl full and leave plenty on the trees.'

Today the garden is maintained by the Charleston Trust and welcomes thousands of visitors every year. It retains a certain looseness that was evident in Bell's descriptions of the spaces she created in the early 20th century (evocatively, in 1936 she wrote that the garden was 'simply a dithering blaze of flowers, butterflies and apples'). To the rear of the house, the garden is walled to enclose long borders surrounding a lawn. In summer, the planting is a romantic tapestry of roses, hollyhocks (*Alcea rosea*), salvias and annuals, and it is easy to imagine that nothing has, in fact, changed since Bell left.

It feels terribly obvious to say that colour was central to life at Charleston, but, for me, its impact on what makes this legacy so romantic cannot be underestimated. When I think about the lives that were lived there, it is impossible to separate the domestic from the artistic. Fixtures and fittings painted in earthy pinks, ochres, murky greens and rusticated reds became not only the backdrop to the pursuit of ideas and creative expression, but also to the most ordinary and functional of daily activities (like washing, eating and sleeping). Through this world of colour, there is a sense of joy in the everyday, a sensibility that places as much value on the art of living as it does on the pursuit of art itself.

Opposite: The hallway at Charleston, restrained and pared back in contrast to the rest of the interior. Bright, sunshine-yellow daffodils offer a burst of vibrant colour that foreshadows the festival of colour to be found throughout the rooms beyond. Overleaf, from left to right: In the acid-green bathroom, daffodils are displayed on a charming, painted side table; outside the doors of Vanessa Bell's bedroom, which open out onto the garden.

A Love Letter to the Cottage Garden
Beth Tarling

COLOUR PROFILE:
Antiqued ruby, bygone pinks and forgotten violets.
A timeworn froth of powdery mauves, bronzed ambers and seductive scarlets.

Hidden down a tiny, winding lane running parallel to the Cornish coast, the home of Beth and Dan Tarling is a dreamscape of floral romance. There are no rules here, no prevailing sense of restraint or restrictive order. Instead, there is only a glorious surrender to the informality of the surrounding maritime landscape. The garden wraps around the 18th-century house, so that you always feel enveloped by a comforting assembly of colour, scent, shape and texture. This is a place where no space is wasted: masses of sweet peas (*Lathyrus odoratus*) rise from clouds of roses; dahlias jostle with annuals, including zinnias, scabious, snapdragons (*Antirrhinum majus*) and cosmos; glasshouses teem with *Calendula* and pelargoniums. All around, there is a sense of abundance – it is a place cultivated to indulge the gardener's every whim and fancy.

Inspiration has come from gardeners in history: Harry Dodson's kitchen garden, the photography of Valerie Finnis, the writing of Candida Lycett Green. All share a common thread, a certain sensitivity to the land and an abstract sense that through gardens they belong to a world made softer and less marred by the brutality of modern life.

Opposite: *Lathyrus odoratus* 'Queen Alexandra' – an old, delicately scented sweet pea in glorious red. Overleaf, from left to right: *L. o.* 'Queen Alexandra' displayed in the boot room against lively red walls; a scrapbook of Cornwall. The gentle and informal decoration of Beth's cottage means it never disrupts the glorious coastal landscape within which it sits.

There is no boundary between the garden and the house. Rather the planting appears to float from beds and borders onto windowsills, tables and cabinets – providing little moments of garden drama dotted everywhere inside. Collections of terracotta pots, old books, china and other curiosities dance around the displays of cut flowers in a way that fills the home with a layered and romantic sense of individuality. Beth traces her interest in the indoor seasonal display of garden blooms back to her mother, who 'always has something from the garden on the kitchen table'. These displays are unfussy; the priority is always to reflect rather simply what is happening outside in the garden, regardless of whether there is a bounty or an off-season scarcity. As Beth describes, 'a few interesting leaves in winter are as much treasured as glorious summer blooms'.

The romance here comes not only from the assembling of plants and objects, but also from Beth and Dan's sense of endeavour. It is the love that is poured into the garden, the hours spent sowing seeds, propagating, cutting back and tying in. It is the memories attached to the artefacts that adorn shelves, hang on walls and sit on coffee tables. Their fingerprints are over everything, and this not only makes their home highly idiosyncratic, but also wonderfully charming.

Colour is embraced; there is no shying away from the most saturated hues. Dahlias in dazzling primary yellow (like 'Kelvin Floodlight') rub shoulders with sweet peas in deep reds ('Queen Alexandra') and *Calendula* in burned orange. Pelargoniums in a myriad of pinks feel just as at home as the sunflowers (*Helianthus*) that range from maroon to the brightest tangerine. The palette is varied and extensive, and while in many respects the colours that Beth and Dan favour lean more towards the energetic, it is the ways in which they are layered with a casual sense of informality both in the garden and in the house that firmly establishes this place as indisputably romantic.

Above: Charming handwritten garden labels in Beth's garden room. Opposite: Dahlias in the most arresting yellow displayed in old horticultural show vases. Large-flowered 'Kelvin Floodlight' is a Decorative cultivar that brings a playful note to the cottage garden.

Romantic Flower Colour
Pink and Purple

Romantic colour is among the most iconic. For many people, including myself, it is pinks and purples that often first come to mind when thinking of a fairy-tale garden: trellises billowing with roses in salmon; salvias and hydrangeas in mysterious plums; Oriental lilies and hollyhocks (*Alcea rosea*) in blush. These are colours to get lost in, fantasy pigments that fill daydreams.

On the surface, flowers in pinks and purples invariably have an overall softness and grace, but this usually masks the true complexity of their character. Pink that leans more to fushia (such as *Dahlia* 'Ambition') has an intense and luxurious feel when compared to a more ethereal pink leaning to blue (like *Geranium* 'Patricia'). A purple dominated by blue feels polished and clean (*Aster* × *frikartii* 'Mönch'), while a purple approaching red feels sensual and seductive (*Rosa* 'Tuscany Superb'). In the flower world, there is really no such thing as a definitive pink and an archetypal purple. Instead, I would argue that there are only degrees to which they radiate romance.

I do think, however, that both colours share an inherent naivety. Regardless of the tint, tone or shade, pink and purple never fail to capture a feeling of innocence and credulity that reminds me of being a carefree child. I suppose a part of everything I do with the garden and with cut flowers is always looking to recreate the cocoon of childhood, to find again that space where life feels uncomplicated and full of possibility. It is perhaps for this reason above all else that these two colours forever fascinate me. They are somehow lost to another age; I see them through a hazy veil of nostalgia.

Over the centuries, successive generations of horticulturists have, like me, found themselves beguiled by the depth and intricacy of pink and purple and taken to obsessive breeding of novel flower cultivars that bloom in every possible permutation of the two. You need only thumb through a rose catalogue to notice the endless pages of pinks, everything from the breathiest almost-whites to the most saccharine bubble-gum pink. A sweet pea catalogue would be much the same when it comes to purple. The danger when faced with so much choice is that we become blasé about just how special flowers in these colours are; their mystery diminished by their ubiquity. I hate to think that I would ever become indifferent to the beauty of a bearded iris (*Iris germanica*), with standards and falls painted in deep amethyst, or a foxglove (*Digitalis purpurea*) splattered with magenta. This is why it is so important for me to remember always that for every blush-pink rose on every summer's day, there must also be a winter of grey.

Pink

Mid-summer is the season of pink. Roses are the most conspicuous at this time of year, but foxgloves, phloxes, penstemons, valerians, thalictrums and poppies all join the pink parade as days reach their longest. It is a colour you can hardly imagine the garden without, a colour so ubiquitous with the idea of romance.

Pink flowers are playful and coy. It is a colour that almost feels unable to take itself seriously, toying with you like a mischievous court jester. This sense of fun is wonderfully distracting and, for me, utterly addictive; no matter how much pink I pack into the garden or the vase, it never feels quite enough. Its colour wheel complement is green, which perhaps explains why it feels so at home. It melts into a surrounding tapestry of verdant foliage with such effortlessness that the two colours often feel inseparable. An enduring and unbreakable marriage.

Part of pink's allure comes from its complexity; no two pinks could ever be the same. As the examples that follow illustrate, it is a colour that can be dressed up or dressed down – sometimes sophisticated, sometimes outright garish.

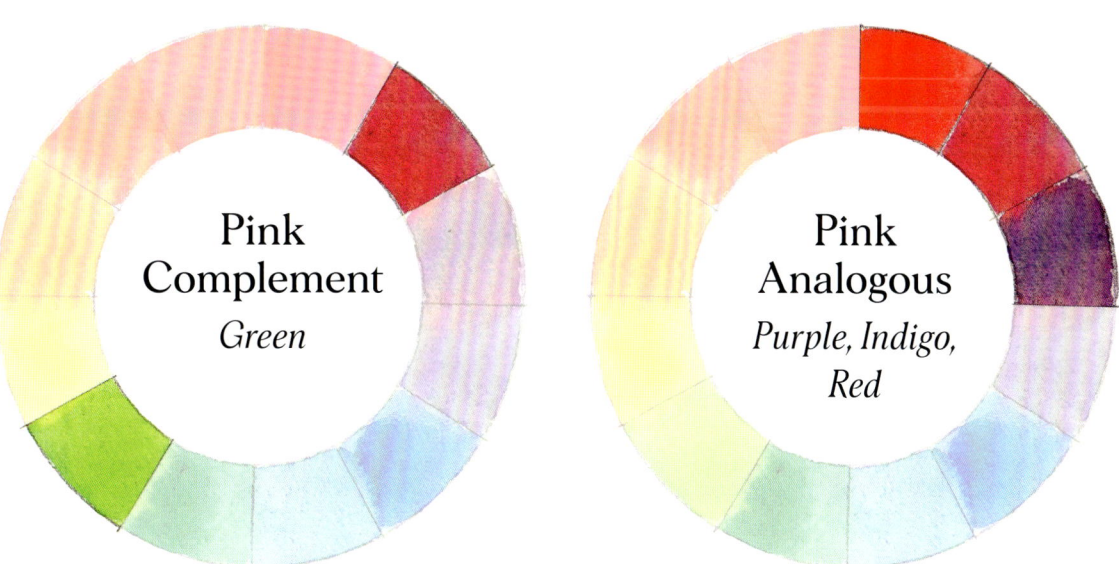

Page 72: The enduring romance of pink and purple. No other garden colours have quite the same ability to take me out of the predictable everyday. Here, the salmon-pink of *Rosa* 'Albertine' and the fizzing candy floss of *R.* Boscobel ('Auscousin') tumble from a Moro Dabron vase on a little table in the garden.
Opposite: Pink scrapbook.

ATMOSPHERE 1: ROMANTIC

Plant Profiles: Candy Pink

The colour of sweet dreams and the breezy buoyancy of youth. Garden candy.

Cosmos bipinnatus 'Candyfloss Pink Sunrise'

Annual • Summer to autumn • Height: up to 60cm (24in), spread: up to 50cm (20in) • Full sun to partial shade • All soil types • Vase life: good (up to 1 week) • Flower colour value: mid

There are plants, like the annual cosmos, that extend early summer's dreamworld of pink further into the year as the garden heads into autumn. The cultivar 'Candyfloss Pink Sunrise' is a particular favourite for its two-tone colouring. At the centre of the flower is a ring of the most intense cerise around an eye of amber stamens (an unexpected, but quite delightful, pairing), from which petals extend in an exciting wash of bubble-gum pink. In large groups, the flowers appear like a dreamy constellation of sugary stars.

Planting note: As cut-and-come again annuals, cosmos are excellent for extending colour in areas of the garden where shrubs and perennials have begun to fade. The looseness of 'Candyfloss Pink Sunrise' looks particularly attractive planted through salvias such as *Salvia* Love and Wishes or penstemons like 'Raven', which both have more upright habits.

In-season complementary colour: *Alchemilla mollis* (chartreuse), *Echinacea purpurea* 'Green Jewel' (chartreuse), *Zinnia elegans* 'Envy' (chartreuse)

In-season analogous colour: *Dahlia* 'Jennifer Mary Ellen' (plum), *Lathyrus odoratus* 'Cedric Morris' (violet-blue), *Salvia nemorosa* 'Caradonna' (violet-purple)

Oenothera lindheimeri Geyser Pink (gaura)

Perennial • Summer • Height: up to 90cm (35in), spread: up to 60cm (24in) • Full sun • All soil types except very heavy clay • Vase life: excellent (1+ week) • Flower colour value: light-to-mid

Oenothera, commonly known as gaura, is an understated plant that adds an understorey of froth to perennial planting. Flowering in a kind of syrupy rosé, this cultivar provides ripples of romantic colour through gaps in beds and in containers for weeks throughout summer and into autumn. Although intense, this pink does not overwhelm its neighbours due to the plant's slouchy habit. Wire-thin stems disperse the colour this way and that, allowing it to undulate through and gently interact with the surrounding planting. Its four-petalled flowers resemble fluttering butterflies as they creep up the plant's fragile stalks.

Planting note: *Oenothera* works well as part of a prairie scheme, where its slender stems are encouraged to float through nearby planting. Grasses, with their similarly informal habit, make attractive companions – the purple moor-grass *Molinia caerulea* subsp. *caerulea* 'Moorhexe' is a good option.

In-season complementary colour: *Angelica archangelica* (chartreuse), *Nicotiana langsdorffii* (chartreuse), *Zinnia elegans* 'Envy' (chartreuse)

In-season analogous colour: *Geranium* × *oxonianum* 'Wargrave Pink' (powder pink), *Rosa* Thomas à Becket ('Auswinston') (ruby), *Salvia nemorosa* 'Sensation Rose' (candy pink)

Rosa Boscobel ('Auscousin')

Perennial, English shrub rose • Summer to autumn (repeat-flowering) • Height: up to 1.5m (5ft), spread: up to 1m (39in) • Full sun to partial shade • All soil types • Vase life: good (up to 1 week) • Flower colour value: mid

Rosa Boscobel was bred by David Austin Roses and introduced in 2012. An English shrub variety, this rose is planted in the courtyard of my London flat. The flowers are medium-sized and the scent is very pleasant, but, for me, the real draw is the compelling colour. It is the sort of deep cerise that grabs you by the scruff of the neck and pulls you in. The colour is multifaceted in the centre of the flower, but from there radiate petals that progressively lighten to create a soft coral halo. Cut by the bucket-load and taken to my cottage in Somerset, *Rosa* Boscobel signals the real start of summer to me.

Planting note: With annual pruning, *Rosa* Boscobel grows into a multistemmed shrub that looks attractive underplanted with shade-tolerant perennials like hardy geraniums and *Tiarella*. *Geranium* × *oxonianum* 'Wargrave Pink' looks particularly romantic emerging in waves underneath the rose's canopy.

In-season complementary colour: *Alchemilla mollis* (chartreuse), *Angelica archangelica* (chartreuse), *Euphorbia amygdaloides* var. *robbiae* (chartreuse)

In-season analogous colour: *Lilium regale* (candy pink-ivory), *Nepeta racemosa* 'Walker's Low' (violet-blue), *Rosa* The Ancient Mariner ('Ausoutcry') (powder pink)

Tulipa 'Columbus'

Perennial bulb (often treated as an annual) • Spring • Height: up to 40cm (16in), spread: up to 30cm (12in) • Full sun to partial shade • All soil types except very heavy clay • Vase life: excellent (1+ week) • Flower colour value: mid

'Columbus' is an early-flowering tulip with extraordinarily showy, peony-like, double flowers. Its ruffled petals cascade from white- and apricot-tinged tips to a deep and mysterious magenta, creating a flower that has a real sense of depth. This tulip provides an early extravagance that foreshadows everything still to come in the garden – the roses, the peonies, the bearded iris (*Iris germanica*) – and inside, when cut for the house, it brings an echo of summer that is most welcome at a time when days are still liable to be cold and nights, although lengthening, still draw in that bit too soon.

Planting note: With its distinctive double flowers, 'Columbus' creates a point of difference in a tulip display. It pairs well with other pink tulips that do not look to compete with its showiness – 'Pink Sound', 'Light and Dreamy' and 'Mistress' are good examples.

In-season complementary colour: *Euphorbia amygdaloides* var. *robbiae* (chartreuse), *Euphorbia epithymoides* (chartreuse), *Helleborus viridis* (chartreuse)

In-season analogous colour: *Fritillaria meleagris* (mid-purple), *Helleborus* × *hybridus* 'Pretty Ellen Spotted' (dark pink), *Muscari* 'Pink Sunrise' (powder pink)

Plant Profiles: Grown-Up Pink

*Seductive and mature, this is pink at its most grown-up.
The garden at peak romance.*

Anemone × hybrida 'Robustissima' (Japanese anemone)

Perennial • Late summer to autumn • Height: up to 1.5m (5ft), spread: up to 1m (39in) • Full sun to partial shade • All soil types • Vase life: good (up to 1 week) • Flower colour value: light

'Robustissima' is a simple flower, with five frilly petals around a central disc of stamens. The sort of bloom a child might draw from their imagination. In spring, the plant begins to produce an enormous mass of foliage, which, you'd be forgiven for thinking, appears to suggest that the flowers to follow will be of an equally impressive size. Instead, the pale pink flowers are surprisingly petite when they arrive. They rise on slender stems and form clusters, each bloom bobbing on the wind. It is a subtle pink, quite unlike most other plants flowering in late summer, with the rich lemon stamens adding a layer of intrigue. The plant's height makes it an important structural plant at the back of borders or as a central feature in containers.

Planting note: 'Robustissima' looks attractive alongside wispy and ethereal grasses like *Pennisetum advena* 'Rubrum', where its tall stems appear to float through the loose foliage.

In-season complementary colour: *Echinacea purpurea* 'Green Jewel' (chartreuse), *Nicotiana langsdorffii* (chartreuse), *Zinnia elegans* 'Envy' (chartreuse)

In-season analogous colour: *Dahlia* 'Arthur Hambley' (candy pink), *Filipendula rubra* 'Venusta' (powder pink), *Monarda* 'Cambridge Scarlet' (mid-red)

Astrantia major 'Star of Love' (masterwort)

Perennial • Summer • Height: up to 1m (39in), spread: up to 1m (39in) • Full sun to partial shade • All soil types except light, sandy soils where moisture retention is poor • Vase life: good (up to 1 week) • Flower colour value: mid-to-dark

Astrantias are excellent plants for areas of dappled summer shade. Growing from neat mounds of foliage, the stems reach around 1m (39in) and support pretty, pincushion flowers with star-shaped bottoms. 'Star of Love' is one of the more richly coloured cultivars, flowering in an evocative deep cerise that almost approaches burgundy. This is the colour of seduction, a sultry and self-aware kind of pink that evokes images of passionate love affairs. There are more show-stopping summer flowers, but perhaps none as intimate as this.

Planting note: In a site in partial shade, ferns such as *Dryopteris affinis* 'Cristata' and *Asplenium trichomanes* look particularly attractive alongside *Astrantia* 'Star of Love'. *Epimedium* foliage also adds an interesting texture.

In-season complementary colour: *Alchemilla mollis* (chartreuse), *Euphorbia epithymoides* (chartreuse), *Zinnia elegans* 'Envy' (chartreuse)

In-season analogous colour: *Digitalis purpurea* 'Sutton's Apricot' (pink-apricot), *Lathyrus odoratus* 'Cupani' (violet-blue), *Rosa* 'Souvenir du Docteur Jamain' (merlot)

Dahlia 'Maldini'

Perennial • Late summer to autumn • Height: up to 1m (39in), spread: up to 1m (39in) • Full sun • All soil types • Vase life: excellent (1+ week) • Flower colour value: mid

'Maldini' is a Decorative dahlia, a category characterized by showy, double flowers and the absence of a central disc of stamens. With geometric perfection, 'Maldini' radiates pointed petals that are at first flushed with pink, but then fade to white at the edges. The tips of the petals are dipped in the tiniest amount of amber to complete the spectacle. This is a dahlia that manages to straddle the divide between classy and flamboyant. For those who find the brightest dahlias a little too brash, but still enjoy the complexity of their shapes, this is perhaps the perfect cultivar.

Planting note: Surrounding 'Maldini' with annual pink *Cosmos bipinnatus* 'Sensation Pinkie' or 'Rubinato' (which both grow to around two-thirds of the height of 'Maldini') creates a thrilling analogous spectacle on two levels.

In-season complementary colour: *Echinacea purpurea* 'Green Jewel' (chartreuse), *Echinops sphaerocephalus* 'Arctic Glow' (ivory-green), *Moluccella laevis* (mid-green)

In-season analogous colour: *Bistorta amplexicaulis* 'Fat Domino' (raspberry), *Salvia nemorosa* 'Sensation Rose' (candy pink), *Sanguisorba hakusanensis* 'Lilac Squirrel' (lilac-powder pink)

Rosa 'Albertine'

Perennial, rambling rose • Summer (once-flowering) • Height: up to 8m (26ft), spread: 4m (13ft) • Full sun to partial shade • All soil types except very heavy clay • Vase life: fair (1–2 days) • Flower colour value: light-to-mid

'Albertine' is a vigorous rambling rose, climbing to around 8m (26ft) if conditions are favourable and suitable support is in place. This is a rose first introduced in the early 20th century, and of all the softer pink varieties, it has to be my absolute favourite. Its flowers are loosely double, giving it an informal and slightly windswept appearance that feels unmistakably romantic – blousy without being completely over the top. The petals are soft pastel pink; there are moments of pure baby pink that melt into salmon and peach.

Planting note: 'Albertine' flowers once in midsummer, so to extend interest it is often a good idea to grow other climbing plants through it – jasmine and clematis work well.

In-season complementary colour: *Alchemilla mollis* (chartreuse), *Angelica archangelica* (chartreuse), *Euphorbia amygdaloides* var. *robbiae* (chartreuse)

In-season analogous colour: *Centranthus ruber* (mid-red), *Gladiolus communis* subsp. *byzantinus* (cerise), *Lupinus* 'Gallery Pink' (mid-pink)

Purple

Purple is the colour of fantasy: evoking hypnotic dreamlands that belong to characters from fairy tales. The intrigue of purple, I think, comes from its blended parentage – part red, part blue. It is halfway between two colours that offer disparate moods: where red is passionate, aggressive and assertive, blue is calming, trustworthy and recuperative. This suspends purple in a state of ambiguity: to which family does it belong? Should we read purple as sensual and provocative or as relaxing and dependable? It is an enigma.

As a flower colour, purple's vagueness enhances a feeling of romance. Drifts of lilac, mauve and violet are a temptation, a mystery waiting to be solved. They soften the more electric tones in the garden and offer a certain level of sophistication that other colours cannot match. Purples also somehow manage to add an instant sense of heritage, as though this planting had been in quiet development for many years, even if it is newly installed; there is a maturity to purple.

Purple's complement is yellow, which, as one of the more divisive flower colours, means that this is often an underexplored partnership in both the garden and the vase. It is perhaps best achieved in spring, when plants like tulips, daffodils, *Iris reticulata* and crocus provide an opportunity to trial the mixing of bulbs in these two colours.

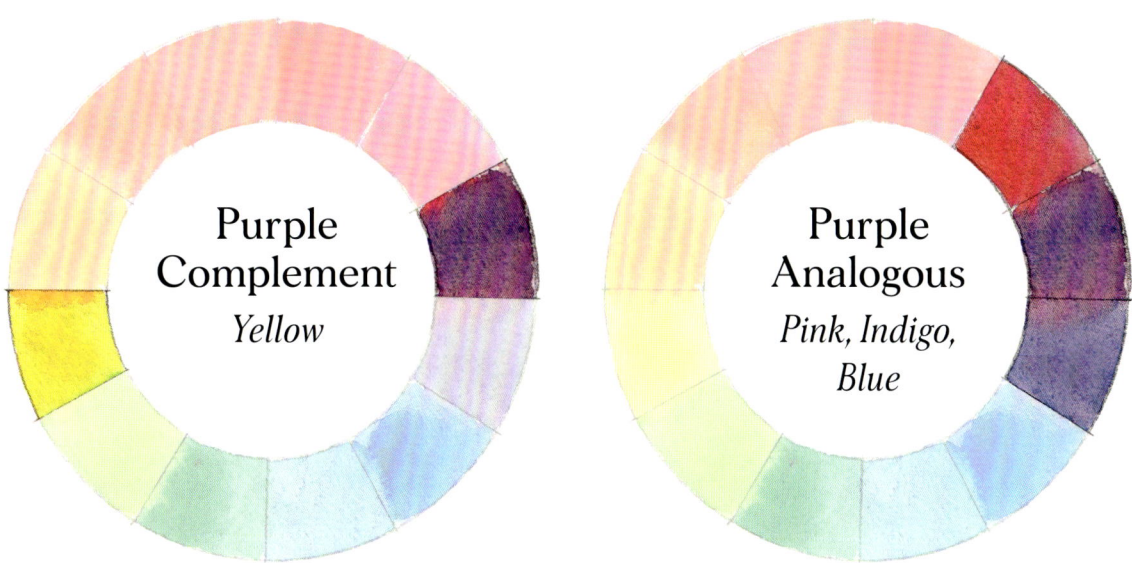

Purple Complement
Yellow

Purple Analogous
Pink, Indigo, Blue

Opposite: Purple scrapbook. There is a mystery to purple – a certain alchemy – that travels through the garden year from the first crocus in spring to the final *Scabiosa atropurpurea* 'Black Knight' in autumn.

Plant Profiles: Mysterious Purple
The purple of intrigue and temptation.
Indulgent colours that transport you into sumptuous fairy tales.

Crocus tommasinianus

Perennial bulb • Spring • Height: up to 10cm (4in), spread: up to 10cm (4in) • Full sun • All soil types • Vase life: fair (1–2 days) • Flower colour value: mid

I seek a pared-back romance inside my cottage throughout winter. Forced bulbs and the odd branch bearing catkins will do. I slip into a quieter world that temporarily becomes a blissful respite from the excesses of the previous year. But one morning I will notice that all the crocuses are starting to arrive, and suddenly the idea of flowers opens before me again. *Crocus tommasinianus* is perhaps one of the most evocative. An astonishing Parma violet, it seems impossible that something so sugary could be born from a landscape still so monochrome. Yet there it is: a chink of light in a tunnel that before seemed endless. The flowers may be tiny, but, at a time when everything else has largely disappeared, they have a grandiose quality and are the start of something quite romantic.

Planting note: *Crocus tommasinianus* looks attractive in drifts through areas of grass. Its colour works well mixed through white varieties such as *C.* 'Jeanne d'Arc' and *C.* 'Ivory Princess'.

In-season complementary colour: *Narcissus* 'February Gold' (mid-yellow), *Primula veris* (mid-yellow), *Primula vulgaris* (butter-yellow)

In-season analogous colour: *Iris reticulata* 'J.S. Dijt' (mid-purple), *Muscari armeniacum* 'Valerie Finnis' (sky-blue), *Scilla forbesii* (sky-blue)

Fritillaria meleagris (snake's head fritillary)

Perennial bulb • Spring • Height: up to 30cm (12in), spread: up to 10cm (4in) • Full sun to partial shade • All soil types • Vase life: good (up to 1 week) • Flower colour value: mid

In a spring garden full of bulbs, it is hard to think of any with a greater sense of whimsical abandon than the fritillary. Fritillaries feel as if they do not belong to us, seeming to have wandered carelessly out of a fairy tale and never made it home. In many ways, *Fritillaria meleagris* is the ultimate flower: very pretty, slightly eccentric, reliable, hardy, long-lasting – both in the garden and cut for the house – pollinator-friendly, and generous in the way it multiplies over time. There is much to love, but, for me, its colour is the most captivating feature. This purple is rich and complex, a dance of plums and lilacs that criss-cross forming the iconic chequerboard pattern decorating every petal. Where most spring bulbs wear their colour loudly, *Fritillaria meleagris* stands out for its demure pigmentation.

Planting note: *Fritillaria meleagris* naturalizes quickly. Together with the white *F. meleagris* var. *unicolor* subvar. *alba*, it looks particularly attractive in drifts through long grass.

In-season complementary colour: *Narcissus* 'Eaton Song' (mid-yellow), *Primula vulgaris* (butter-yellow), *Tulipa* 'Daydream' (apricot-tangerine)

In-season analogous colour: *Helleborus* × *hybridus* 'Pretty Ellen Pink' (powder pink), *Iris reticulata* 'Blue Note' (mid-blue), *Muscari aucheri* 'Blue Magic' (powder blue)

Iris germanica 'Prince of Burgundy' (bearded iris)

Perennial • Late spring • Height: up to 50cm (20in), spread: up to 50cm (20in) • Full sun • All soil types except very heavy clay • Vase life: good (up to 1 week) • Flower colour value: mid-to-dark

Always the first bearded iris to flower in my garden in late spring, 'Prince of Burgundy' has a quiet luxury that signals a delightful change of pace following the riot of spring bulbs. Its standards (the upright petals) and falls (the drooping petals) are a wonderfully deep, antique purple and quite unlike other colours in my garden. It is a seductive colour, rich and velvety. Petals give way to a creamy white at their centre – leaving behind only a speckling of purple – before a beard in brilliant orange extends from the throat. There is mystique here, a sense that this flower has journeyed from somewhere quite palatial and found itself in my garden.

Planting note: The darkness of 'Prince of Burgundy' works well planted beside lighter pinks, purples and even soft blues in a romantic scheme. *Geranium* Dreamland (which has adorable powder-pink flowers) or *Nepeta racemosa* 'Walker's Low' (with sprightly blue-mauve flowers) is a good place to start.

In-season complementary colour: *Primula veris* (mid-yellow), *Rosa* Lady of Shalott ('Ausnyson') (apricot), *Rosa* Roald Dahl ('Ausowlish') (butter-apricot)

In-season analogous colour: *Centranthus ruber* (mid-red), *Lupinus* 'Gallery Pink' (mid-pink), *Rosa* Boscobel ('Auscousin') (candy pink)

Rosa Munstead Wood ('Ausbernard')

Perennial, English shrub rose • Summer to autumn (repeat-flowering) • Height: up to 1.5m (5ft), spread: up to 1m (39in) • Full sun to partial shade • All soil types • Vase life: good (up to 1 week) • Flower colour value: mid-to-dark

Rosa Munstead Wood was bred by David Austin Roses in 2007 and named after the Surrey home of English garden writer and designer Gertrude Jekyll. Cupped, deeply ruffled flowers are distinctly old-rose in appearance, and like an Old Master's meticulously mixed oils, the colour has a mesmerizing depth. It is a rich scarlet-purple, the colour of Pinot Noir: intense at the edges, becoming more effervescent in the centre. It feels like pure indulgence and offers a sophisticated alternative to early summer's abundance of pink roses. It grows into a bushy and spreading structural plant with a strong, fruity perfume.

Planting note: The dark, enigmatic colour looks attractive mixed through softer varieties in a mixed rose border. The charmingly blousy *Rosa* Emily Brontë ('Ausearnshaw') makes a good neighbour, as does the delicate, pink-peach of *Rosa* The Shepherdess ('Austwist').

In-season complementary colour: *Iris germanica* 'Benton Apollo' (lemon-yellow), *Iris germanica* 'Old Hall' (tangerine), *Rosa* Roald Dahl ('Ausowlish') (butter-apricot)

In-season analogous colour: *Allium hollandicum* 'Purple Sensation' (mid-purple), *Digitalis purpurea* 'Dalmatian Rose' (mauve), *Geranium* 'Blushing Turtle' (powder pink)

Plant Profiles: Purple, Almost Black

A cloak of mystery, an enigma. Murky corridors of an old museum in the dead of night. The colour of ambiguity.

Lathyrus odoratus 'Beaujolais' (sweet pea)

Annual • Summer • Height: up to 1.8m (6ft), spread: up to 50cm (20in) • Full sun • All soil types except very heavy clay • Vase life: good (up to 1 week) • Flower colour value: dark

The quintessential cottage garden flower, sweet peas bring some timeworn glamour to early summer. Found in a dizzying array of colours – everything from breathy whites and mauves to intense reds and oranges – perhaps the most beguiling are those that are so rich they almost appear black. 'Beaujolais' has a distinct plum pigmentation in bright sunshine, but in duller conditions, its true mystery is revealed. Suddenly cloaked in a veil of ambiguity, 'Beaujolais' appears to have transformed into pure charcoal. The ability to travel between light and dark – hope and despair – together with its intoxicating perfume imbues this flower with endless intrigue.

Planting note: 'Beaujolais' is best grown up a wigwam or trellis. Its floriferous performance looks most romantic when emerging from early summer planting in a mixed bed or border. Its flowering is prolonged by frequent deadheading.

In-season complementary colour: *Achillea filipendulina* 'Cloth of Gold' (mid-yellow), *Phlomis russeliana* (lemon-butter), *Rosa* Roald Dahl ('Ausowlish') (butter-apricot)

In-season analogous colour: *Astilbe chinensis* 'Dunes Future' (lilac), *Nepeta racemosa* 'Walker's Low' (violet-blue), *Rosa* Munstead Wood ('Ausbernard') (merlot)

Primula 'Silver Lace Black'

Perennial • Spring • Height: up to 20cm (8in), spread: up to 30cm (12in) • Full sun to partial shade • All soil types • Vase life: good (up to 1 week) • Flower colour value: dark

Emerging in early spring, 'Silver Lace Black' is an extraordinarily attractive primula. The flowers appear in handsome clusters with petals that are a deep, mesmerizing purple edged with a contrasting, off-white border. An egg-yolk-yellow centre completes the drama. Although small in size, the flowers' performance is truly fanciful, and they add an element of playfulness to a spring garden mostly dominated by flamboyant bulbs. It is their eccentricity that I find most charming – they have an air of romantic individualism.

Planting note: *Primula* 'Silver Lace Black' is excellent in a container and looks particularly attractive in small terracotta pots as part of a wider group. They are perfect for 'theatre' displays that may also contain auriculas (*Primula auricula*).

In-season complementary colour: *Narcissus* 'February Gold' (mid-yellow), *Primula veris* (mid-yellow), *Primula vulgaris* (butter-yellow)

In-season analogous colour: *Helleborus × hybridus* 'Pretty Ellen Spotted' (powder pink), *Iris reticulata* 'J.S. Dijt' (mid-purple), *Tulipa* 'Columbus' (cerise)

Scabiosa atropurpurea 'Black Knight'

Perennial • Summer to autumn • Height: up to 1m (39in), spread: up to 50cm (20in) • Full sun • All soils except very heavy clay • Vase life: excellent (1+ week) • Flower colour value: dark

'Black Knight' is a show-stopping scabious that, with regular deadheading and cutting for the house, flowers over summer and into autumn. The intense burgundy, pincushion flowers appear hauntingly black from afar. Up close, the colour nuance is revealed: the flower centres are darkest, creating shadowy voids that the surrounding lighter petals – in a rich, velvety cherry – seem lost to. The impression is one of a brooding, almost melancholy, flower, but for me this adds an interesting colour texture to the romantic garden. It offers a moment of mystery amid the blousy pinks and lighter purples, and as a filler in perennial planting allows the eye a moment of rest.

Planting note: This scabious looks best drifting through mixed summer planting where it provides dark accents against lighter-coloured flowers. It is particularly attractive paired with plants that have an upright, but loose, habit like *Penstemon* 'Hidcote Pink' and *Nepeta racemosa* 'Walker's Low'.

In-season complementary colour: *Cosmos bipinnatus* 'Xanthos' (lemon-butter), *Dahlia* 'Bishop of York' (mid-yellow), *Helianthus* 'Lemon Queen' (mid-yellow)

In-season analogous colour: *Cosmos bipinnatus* 'Candyfloss Pink Sunrise' (candy pink), *Dahlia* 'Ambition' (cerise-purple), *Salvia nemorosa* 'Caradonna' (violet-purple)

Tulipa 'Continental'

Perennial bulb (often treated as an annual) • Spring • Height: up to 50cm (20in), spread: up to 50cm (20in) • Full sun to partial shade • All soils except very heavy clay • Vase life: excellent (1+ week) • Flower colour value: dark

In a garden like mine where tulips come thick and fast in all manner of ostentatious pinks, yellows, reds and oranges, it is often a welcome breath of fresh air to see a container of 'Continental'. A Triumph Group tulip, 'Continental' is demure where other tulips look for the spotlight; it is self-assured of its own beauty. The flowers are cup-shaped in a deep and glossy mahogany-purple, which at dawn and dusk appears black. The stems, which rise from gently crimped leaves, seem to mirror the flower's moodiness in a dark grey-green. This is a tulip that adds sophistication and opulence to the spring bulb display.

Planting note: 'Continental' pairs well with vibrant mid-purples in a tulip display – 'Bleu Aimable', 'Kansas Proud', 'Merlot' and 'Ballade' make attractive neighbours.

In-season complementary colour: *Iris germanica* 'Benton Apollo' (lemon-yellow), *Iris germanica* 'Old Hall' (tangerine), *Primula veris* (mid-yellow)

In-season analogous colour: *Helleborus* × *hybridus* 'Pretty Ellen Spotted' (powder pink), *Muscari armeniacum* 'Valerie Finnis' (sky-blue), *Tiarella* 'Pink Skyrocket' (salmon)

Beyond Romanticism

Pink and purple are so irresistible in the romance they bring to the garden and the vase that they are often enough on their own to create compelling spectacles of colour. However, the most surprising and enigmatic compositions are born from the introduction of colours outside the romantic family. The act of bringing together flower colour is one without rules (and, to my mind, at least half the fun is in the exploration of novel pairings), yet there are certain accompaniments to pink and purple that always provoke interest. These combinations may at first seem unusual, but they have the capacity for magic in a way that only flowers can.

Soft Yellow

Among the brightest pinks and purples, softer yellows can become lost. Not quite white, they do not benefit from white's luminous ability to cut through the loudness of the romantic performance. An example in tulips would be the buttery 'Elegant Lady' mixed through the electric 'Pink Impression' and 'Kansas Proud'. Here, the delicacy and nuance of 'Elegant Lady' is likely to be eclipsed by the melee of its neighbours. However, softer yellows mixed through groups of flowers in a more muted coral or powdery mauve has the ability to heighten a sense of romance. Continuing with the example of 'Elegant Lady', perhaps a better match would be 'Salmon Impression' and 'Gabriella', a combination of pastels that together sing in dreamy unison.

Powder Blue

As with softer yellows, powdery blue can elevate quieter pinks and purples in a romantic scheme. It is the dusty almost-mauves of *Geranium* Rozanne, *Muscari armeniacum* 'Valerie Finnis' and *Iris* × *robusta* 'Gerald Darby' – blues that are sugary and take their cues from violet. When mixed through corals and salmons, these blues create a sense of nostalgia; they bring to mind timeworn cottage gardens where planting has been left – or indeed encouraged – to effortlessly coalesce in loose waves of mixed colour groups.

Acid-Green

With the most brash and flamboyant pinks and purples, the acidity of chartreuse often makes a pleasing contrast (and it is, indeed, hot pink's complement on the colour wheel). The sprightly viridescence of flowers like *Alchemilla mollis*, *Euphorbia amygdaloides* var. *robbiae* and *Zinnia elegans* 'Envy' cut through the most candied tones in a way that could perhaps only be matched, but not bettered, by pure white. Acid-green is a colour that seems to curiously bounce off its loud counterparts, while at the same time melting into them – a quite perfect harmony is established. The acidity tempers the sweetness of the romantic tones; it brings a sense of grounding to an otherwise rather fanciful composition.

Opposite: Soft and buttery roses – 'Ghislaine de Féligonde', 'Julia's Rose' and A Shropshire Lad ('Ausled') – are mixed through a palette of pinks. Rather than distracting from the sense of romance, these creamy varieties enhance the mood.

Illustrative Romantic Planting Plan

Roses anchor this romantic planting plan: the indulgent claret of *Rosa* Munstead Wood ('Ausbernard') to the left, the raspberry ripple of rosa mundi (*Rosa gallica* 'Versicolor') towards the centre-front, and the vibrant candy pink of *Rosa* Boscobel ('Auscousin') to the right. Not only do they bring moments of blousy interest, but they also provide height at three key intersections of the scheme.

Rosa Munstead Wood emerges through floaty drifts of *Oenothera lindheimeri* Geyser Pink and *Alchemilla mollis*, two plants that are bounced liberally through the composition. The chartreuse of *Alchemilla mollis* provides an unexpected colour contrast to the prevailing pinks and purples, allowing the eye to rest, while digesting the surrounding romantic colours. The delicate and informal ripples of oenothera inject a syrupy splash of coral here and there. Both have lighter values than the roses, which creates a thrilling sense of dynamism.

The height of *Rosa gallica* 'Versicolor' is matched by the powder pink of *Anemone* × *hybrida* 'Robustissima' and the brooding purple of *Scabiosa atropurpurea* 'Black Knight'. However, with their more upright habits, both plants create a pleasing textural contrast to the rose's bushy growth. With a darker value than anything else in the composition, the 'Black Knight' scabious retreats into the background, creating a shadowy accent.

To the left, *Rosa* Boscobel's height is mirrored by that of *Verbena bonariensis*, but to the right, *Geranium* × *oxonianum* 'Wargrave Pink' allows the composition to softly descend in clouds of breathy pastel. For balance, the geranium also creeps across the right-hand side of the scheme.

Two moments of magic pop through the composition – one towards the back on the left-hand side and one at the front towards the centre – as shots of *Iris germanica* 'Benton Daphne' pierce through the planting in beguiling magenta. Their elegantly elongated shape cuts through the floaty *Oenothera lindheimeri* Geyser Pink, *Alchemilla mollis* and *Geranium* × *oxonianum* 'Wargrave Pink' to reward the eye with architectural contrast, an effect that is mirrored on the right-hand side by the regal lily (*Lilium regale*).

Cosmos bipinnatus 'Candyfloss Pink Sunrise' rounds off the composition. Emerging in a drift at the front, it creates a stepping stone from which *Rosa* Boscobel and *Verbena bonariensis* can climb. Overall, there is an attractive sense of rise and fall, of pinks and purples dancing in romantic unison.

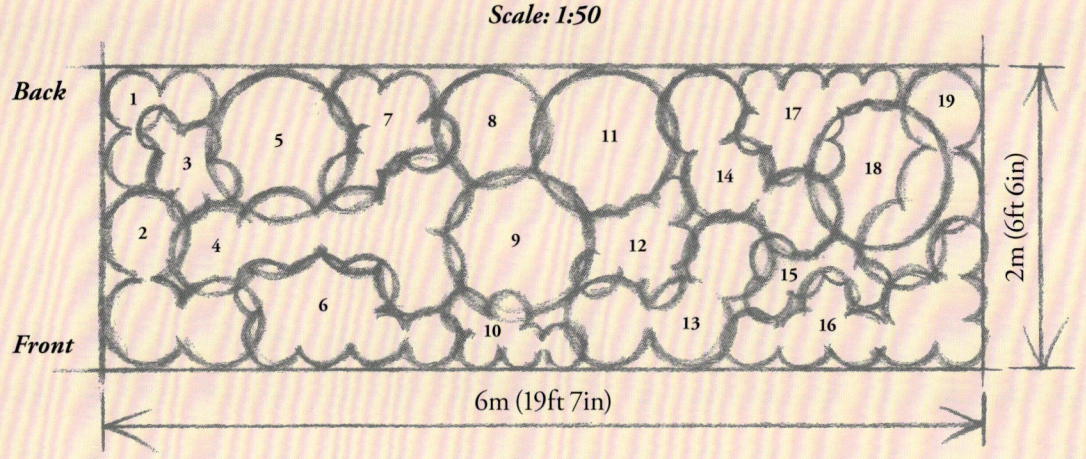

1. *Alchemilla mollis* × 3
2. *Geranium* × *oxonianum* 'Wargrave Pink' × 3
3. *Iris germanica* 'Benton Daphne' × 5
4. *Oenothera lindheimeri* Geyser Pink × 5
5. *Rosa* Munstead Wood ('Ausbernard') × 1
6. *Alchemilla mollis* × 7
7. *Salvia* 'Amistad' × 5
8. *Scabiosa atropurpurea* 'Black Knight' × 1
9. *Rosa gallica* 'Versicolor' × 1
10. *Iris germanica* 'Benton Daphne' × 5
11. *Anemone* × *hybrida* 'Robustissima' × 1
12. *Lilium regale* × 7
13. *Geranium* × *oxonianum* 'Wargrave Pink' × 3
14. *Oenothera lindheimeri* Geyser Pink × 3
15. *Lilium regale* × 5
16. *Cosmos bipinnatus* 'Candyfloss Pink Sunrise' × 9
17. *Verbena bonariensis* × 9
18. *Rosa* Boscobel ('Auscousin') × 1
19. *Geranium* × *oxonianum* 'Wargrave Pink' × 3

Notes

This illustrative planting plan would reach its peak in early to mid-summer and would perform best in full sun. Its season of interest could be extended into spring by scattering through a selection of tulips such as 'Columbus', 'Albert Heijn', 'Flaming Flag' and 'Continental'.

Notes on Romantic Cut Flower Displays

Romantic cut flower displays benefit from a sense of abundance. Garden flowers that collide with one another and spill from a container in a frenzied and haphazard fight for the spotlight. Is it possible to fit in one more stem?

I always want to avoid over-engineering a romantic display, which usually means that the mechanics of holding an arrangement together – like flower frogs and chicken wire – are avoided too. Whenever possible, I prefer to fill a vessel so completely that the flowers effectively hold themselves in place. There is a wonderful simplicity to this sort of composition, a freeing laissez-faire that feels effortless and uncontrived.

The imperfection and informality of flowers in the vase creates a charming naivety, a sense of the flowers having organized themselves, and this is only heightened when a generous mix of textures is used. Fluffy roses bumping into silky irises; powdery geraniums bouncing through glossy sweet peas. The aim is, for me, always to replicate the diversity of forms in the garden, bringing the myriad of petal shapes, leaf structures and stem formations together like a floral exhibition. There is a certain innocence and honesty in clashing textures that I always find terribly romantic; there is no sense of pretension or of the display having been overworked and highly fussed over – the flowers are encouraged to produce their own magic.

Pinks and purples tend to have mid-values, and in a romantic floral display I think they are best showcased when there are one or two darker flowers in the arrangement. In late summer, this might be a brooding dahlia like 'Arabian Night' or 'Dark Spirit'; in spring, it could be a tulip such as 'Continental' or 'Queen of Night'. Anything, really, that creates a sense of depth through the pink and purple mid-ground. The aim is to encourage the eye to pull the arrangement apart, to be able to recognize the constituent parts while appreciating a fanciful whole.

Romantic indoor flowers should follow the seasonal ebb and flow of the garden. There is something distinctly unromantic to me about a vase of roses in the frozen depths of winter or a jug of tulips in the retreating days of autumn; arranged out of season, flowers lose the magic that comes with their wider context in a garden setting. The enchantment of roses, for example, is in part wrapped up in their association with the long, sun-soaked afternoons of high summer as much as it is in their physical beauty. Tulips, although always undeniably pretty, capture a sense of spring's optimism that surely constitutes a large part of their majesty when they arrive early in the year. In this way, it is always so important to me that the flowers I display represent something of the present, a feeling of what is happening right now in the garden and the landscape beyond.

Often, the most romantic displays use the vessel to enhance the magic. The most evocative have a history – recent or old – that adds a layer of interest to the flowers. It might be a favourite childhood cup, an antique jug or simply an old jar of olives that is now recycled for the purpose of arranging flowers. Anything that brings a sense of individualism and personality to the composition. Romanticism is about tying together the whole experience of the display. Of course, the flowers are central to the display, but the container and its setting within the house all play a part too.

Opposite left: The impossibly pretty pairing of tulips 'Ballade' and 'La Belle Époque'. Opposite right: A blousy display of *Rosa* Boscobel ('Auscousin') in a simple antique jug. Above: A riotous handful of garden flowers for a summer picnic in romantic pinks and purples. Subtle, powdery shades are mixed with bright, electric tones to create a display with depth.

Opposite: A fountain of daffodils in the sitting room of my Somerset cottage. Arresting canary yellow colliding with creamy butter and rusted orange, these are the colours I perhaps most look forward to all winter. They have a certain urgency, an immediately uplifting feeling of joy. Above: As spring really gets going, the cheering sunshine-yellow of daffodils begins to populate all available space in my cottage. Here, they welcome me home, parading across a little window.

Atmosphere 2:
Energetic

The excitable haze of a scorched summer's afternoon. The sun, commanding and obstinate, drowning the landscape in a wash of searing light. Parched fields rusting the landscape, sparkling streams flowing through golden woodland. Energetic colour is unmistakable. It is the colour that fills memories of long school holidays and sustains dreams of warmer days during the harshest trials of winter.

I live vicariously through the garden's energy. Where in everyday life I may be introverted, it is with plants and flowers that I feel distinctly gregarious. What I take from the garden is far more than an appreciation of its endless beauty; it is a certain confidence too. A confidence to express myself more freely, to ignore the murmurings of self-doubt. I suppose this is why I am always drawn to bold flower colour; it feels exotic to me, the antithesis of my personality. Perhaps, really, I envy it.

Opposite: Energetic scrapbook. Reds, oranges and yellows not only bring a sense of vitality to the garden but also inspire a certain *joie de vivre* inside me too.

The Rousing Spirit of the Garden

Being energetic is as much a state of mind as it is physical. Plants that collide in a riot of extravagant reds, oranges and yellows awaken ideas and opportunities; they inspire you to be proactive and feed the imagination. This concept was explored by the Fauvist group of artists in the early 20th century. The likes of André Derain and Henri Matisse interrogated the natural world through intense and unrestrained colour, and in so doing they captured a certain *joie de vivre*, a sense of the landscape's unbreakable spirit. Fauvist work was not grounded in realism or concerned with combining colour in a pleasingly aesthetic manner. Rather it sought to represent something more intrinsic and universal than conventional beauty: an energy. Where trees appear in burned oranges in Derain's *L'Estaque*, there is vitality; where foliage becomes teal in *Les Montagnes à Collioure*, there is dynamism; where whole landscapes are painted in pink, purple and red in *Paysage au bord de la Mer*, there is ambition. It is an art movement that I always look to as a key inspiration, reflecting my quest for nature's underlying verve. It is mountains of blazing nasturtiums (*Tropaeolum majus*) on hazel wigwams, containers fizzing with zinnias, cut displays of tulips in feisty reds and plucky yellows. The natural world is teeming with colourful enthusiasm, and within all its fantastical tints, tones and shades I hope to acquire an ounce of that fervour too.

Being energetic in the garden is about never sitting still. It is a thirst for betterment, for trialling something different when a new season comes again.

Opposite: A carnival of tulips in spring. Above left: The marigold *Tagetes tenuifolia* 'Golden Gem'. Above right: The apricot-orange of *Tulipa* 'Lighting Sun'.

One lifetime may not be enough to explore the full breadth of colour that plants give us, but I won't waste a second trying. I suppose in this way the energetic gardener is a scientist, concocting experiments and scrutinizing the results; not everything is successful, but instead of being viewed as a failure, missteps are celebrated as learnings.

I use my garden and the displays I bring into the house like a sketchbook: spaces where combinations of bold colour can be tested. They are personal creative worlds, places that constantly evolve according to the whims of my imagination. However, I suppose where a sketchbook prepares an artist to execute a fully resolved final piece, in my case, no such sense of eventual accomplishment is ever sought. Quite simply, the garden and the house continue in a state of perpetual experimentation; there is never a sense of work having been completed, and this, to me, gives the flowers I grow and display a feeling of everlasting momentum from which I take a tremendous amount of energy. As a cycle of rise and decline – colour in abundance and then in scarcity – it propels me through the year on a wave of expectation.

Colour is central to a garden's energetic performance, but it is not the only actor; the role of texture is, to my mind, a notable element too. Texture is the fabric of a garden or cut flower display, the lattice that holds everything together. It is layers of bristling ferns mixed through the arching stems of Solomon's seal (*Polygonatum × hybridum*) or the floating foliage of ornamental grasses as they ripple between upright and robust coneflowers (*Echinacea*). A diverse mix of texture coupled with a melee of bold colour creates thrilling results. Planting schemes and cut flower displays suddenly become melting pots of ideas as different forms and hues collide. There is movement, dynamism and spirit, and at no point is the eye ever at risk of becoming bored. This is energy at its most immediate and transparent. The kind of high-octane, spirited atmosphere that compels you to join in its exuberance.

∗

Exploring places that exude energy can be quite addictive. I always feel a sense of buoyancy and creative refreshment when visiting homes and gardens that have been put together with vibrancy. It is a feeling that I chase when I find myself uninspired or lacking motivation.

The people and places that feature over the following pages all share this ability to lift the spirits. Theirs are spaces that dazzle with carnivals of colour, texture, and in a way that is more abstract, a sense of freedom.

Opposite, clockwise from top left: A small display of nasturtiums (*Tropaeolum majus*) in energetic orange is sometimes all that is needed to brighten a dull day; tulips, blown out at the point of going over, in loud and uncompromising orange create some of the most arresting displays across the whole year; Icelandic poppies (*Oreomecon nudicaulis*) in yellows and oranges; a petite bowl of daffodils, crocuses and primroses in early spring.

ATMOSPHERE 2: ENERGETIC

Opposite: A bucket of cut flowers in energetic colours at Sarah Wilson's flower farm in Somerset. Dahlias, rudbeckias, zinnias and the French marigold *Tagetes patula* 'Burning Embers' mark late summer's fiery crescendo. Above: Daffodils in old horticultural show vases line the window of my studio.

A Hypnotic Kaleidoscope of Colour
Max Hurd

COLOUR PROFILE:
Incandescent vermillion, earthy mustard and fruity peach.
A saturated carnival.

In northwest London, stylist Max Hurd has created a home that is as personal and idiosyncratic as it is energetic and vibrant. Upon entering, you embark upon a rollercoaster of colour, and what is most immediately striking is just how quickly the beige and monotonous urban streetscape from which you came seems to dissipate from your consciousness. This is a sanctuary for the anti-bland.

The interior is a collaboration between Max and interior decorator Benedict Foley. Friends before they started on the project, the pair understood each other's taste before any scheming began, which, as Max explains, made their combined creative input joyously effortless: 'The process was incredibly natural and easy…he grasped instantly the world I wanted to create for myself.' The result is thrilling and sees the library in a deep and earthy green, the sitting room in zesty vermillion, the kitchen in a seductive peach, and the pantry in citrus-lemon – each one a canvas overlaid with upholstery, antiques, curiosities and keepsakes to create a treasure box of pattern and texture.

Opposite: Deep forest-green walls provide a complementary backdrop for the scarlet red of the common poppy (*Papaver rhoeas*) in Max's library.

For Max, colour is an antidote to the city. 'London is a great place, but living and working here, you are constantly surrounded by a world of bland concrete and grey skies,' he tells me. 'Being able to come home, fling open my front door and lose myself in a vast array of different colours is a huge source of comfort.'

There is certainly a sense of colour as therapy in this home. It is a mood-lifter, a medicine. And this is only amplified by cut flowers, which are always present and an endless source of inspiration to Max. Just like the walls, furniture and objects on display, it is always the most saturated blooms that find their way inside. They feel instantly at home, adding yet another layer to the overall feeling of effervescence. Somehow, bearded irises (*Iris germanica*) feel particularly appropriate, their extravagant standards and falls seeming to luxuriate in the sumptuous surroundings.

But moments of floral restraint offer a pleasing contrast to the interior too. A simple vase of foliage on the kitchen table, a tiny cup of snowdrops (*Galanthus*) on a windowsill; they ground this vibrant space with a sense of the outside world. Thrillingly, their simplicity is pulled into sharp focus in a way that would be lost in a more neutral setting.

There is a small courtyard garden, but on account of it being awkwardly shaded for almost the whole day, Max usually sources his flowers from English growers in London. This means there is always an excitingly unpredictable rotation of blooms coming through the door. One day, it might be roses adding a blousy accent to the lively sitting room, the next it might be delphiniums bolting through the kitchen in electric blues. These constantly changing displays feel in keeping with the infectious energy that radiates from each room, and for Max, they offer tantalizing opportunities to experiment with different ways of arranging. As Max puts it: 'When the vases are empty, I often feel like the house is not quite dressed. Like a great dame going to a ball without her jewellery or a gentleman in evening dress without a bow tie, flowers are the cherry on top of the cake.'

Previous pages, from left to right: A sprawling display of roses in peachy pinks sits playfully against powdery blue walls, furniture and the Nuthall Temple 'Ivy Trellis' fabric in cornflower blue; the exuberance of vermillion in Max's sitting room, with showy bearded irises (*Iris germanica*). Opposite: A simple display of oak leaves in the kitchen. Above: Seductive colours and fantastically flamboyant shapes make bearded irises the perfect accompaniment to Max's interior.

A Sanctuary of Colour
Isabel and Julian Bannerman

COLOUR PROFILE:
Burned red, sparkling orange and honeyed yellow.
Primaries mixed through pastels. A jamboree of colour.

Deep in rural Somerset, down winding lanes that intersect ancient farmland, the home of garden designers Isabel and Julian Bannerman has sat in gentle repose for some five hundred years. Today, the house has a relaxed and mellow elegance, which seems to suggest that nothing much has changed in that half-millennium. But the truth is that upon arriving at Ashington Manor, the Bannermans were faced with a daunting to-do list of repairs and renovations. New floors needed adding; insensitive additions needed removing.

The interiors are generously layered, their Elizabethan bones dressed in tapestries, paintings, books and endless curiosities. While there is a sense of deference to the house's history, this does not suffocate. Instead, the past shines playfully through a fascinating collection of the pair's wide-ranging creative impulses. The result is a feeling of stepping into a world that feels, tantalizingly, like a journey through Isabel and Julian's imagination.

Opposite: Handfuls of lively dahlias, zinnias and French marigolds (*Tagetes patula*) displayed simply in glass vases in Isabel and Julian's kitchen. Their playful colours and shapes add another curious layer to this jewel box of a domestic space.

Previous pages, clockwise from left: The highly energetic froth of *Cosmos sulphureus* in a mochaware jug; a majestic container display of snowy angel's trumpet (*Brugmansia suaveolens*) in the courtyard; blazing drifts of orange Mexican sunflower (*Tithonia rotundifolia*) in mixed borders; potted pink pelargoniums; a cheerful jug of sunflowers (*Helianthus*) and rudbeckias in the pantry. Opposite: *Cosmos* in neon pink adds to the layers of colour and texture in the library.

When inside, a sense of the garden is always close. Open doors offer glimpses of courtyards overflowing with containers of annual interest and mullioned windows look out onto long borders jostling with texture. The two realms – inside and outside – feel inextricably linked, as if one could not exist without the other. There is an energy, a certain sparkling verve, that not only appears to unite the two domains but also permeates through the visitor; an uplifting spirit that brightens anyone who enters.

Outside, the garden is a timeless fairy tale befitting this land's sweeping backstory. From the sunny hall, a keystone arched doorway first leads to a terrace and then to lawns dissected by gravel paths; cylindrical clipped yews anchor the scheme and provide a pleasing structural contrast to the surrounding loose and sprawling borders. Looking east, the topiary leads the eye to a charming 13th-century church that sits just beyond the Manor's boundary, while to the west, an uninterrupted view of open country stretches to the horizon. A large courtyard sits to the rear, which becomes a delightful circus of containers frothing with masses of pelargoniums, annuals and more exotic specimens like potted snowy angel's trumpet (*Brugmansia suaveolens*).

Textures, shapes and scents are layered with thrilling abundance, but, for me, the garden's most intoxicating sensory stimulant is its use of unbridled colour. In one breath, borders combine the electric oranges of the Mexican sunflower *Tithonia rotundifolia* 'Torch' and the rusted reds of *Helenium* 'Moerheim Beauty' with the candied pinks and mysterious purples of phlox. Then in another, pots tumble with the sunshine-yellows of *Tagetes* and the sky-blues of bog sage (*Salvia uliginosa*). Colour, in its unrivalled ability to move the observer in some way, is a thread running through all the Bannermans' work in the garden, a shared love affair with the fantasy dreamworlds that colour has the power to create. As Isabel explains enthusiastically:

'A fearless approach to colour is something Julian and I have shared from our first meeting and something we have both gleaned from the past and from nature – which is always full of surprises and bold beauty.' This is a place that manages to feel both sensitive to the surrounding landscape and somehow like a wonderful escape. The sense is of abandoning the everyday in favour of an enchanting retreat into a highly personal world of energetic floral mania.

Above: A jewel-box mix of zinnias displayed informally in a lustre jug in Isabel and Julian's courtyard. Opposite: Columns of clipped yew perfectly frame a view to the neighbouring church.

An Elegant Flurry of Exuberance
Robin Lucas

COLOUR PROFILE:
*Rusted orange, brooding red and buttery yellows.
A sophisticated and dynamic combination of hearty brights.*

The Ribble Valley in Lancashire offers a fabled image of England: a vast landscape of lush hills dissected by dry-stone walls and little lanes winding through ancient woodland on their way to sleepy villages. A place that feels as if it has been carved from the earth by a 19th-century Romantic poet.

At the heart of this arcadia, hidden within the halcyon fells and valleys of the Forest of Bowland, the home of artist Robin Lucas and his partner Tom provides a gentle spark of creative energy. The house is an early-19th-century mill with a handsome river flowing on one side and a view of open country on the other. This is a place that feels far away from everyday life, a kind of sanctuary reached by a long, anonymous drive that is itself set back from a quiet country lane.

Gardened areas sit in pockets all around the property. To the front, there are full and gregarious cottage beds filled with roses, lilies, phlox and ornamental grasses in summer; to the rear, there are playful container displays of pelargoniums.

Opposite: A late summer mix of dahlias explodes from a decorative urn in Robin's sitting room. Across the house, neutral walls provide the perfect canvas for exuberant cut flowers.

Opposite: Robin's kitchen dresser with an electric display of *Dahlia* 'Gerrie Hoek' mixed with fennel (*Foeniculum vulgare*). Above: Nestled at the bottom of a driveway, Robin's house sits in harmony with the surrounding landscape of the Ribble Valley.

Down towards the river there is a kitchen garden that mixes annuals like marigolds (*Calendula*), nasturtium (*Tropaeolum majus*) and sunflowers (*Helianthus*) with courgettes, beans and fennel (*Foeniculum vulgare*). There is a wonderful sense of enclosure here, a feeling of being swaddled by planting at every turn.

Robin has a background in botany, and it is clear when talking with him that his connection to the garden runs deeper than simply an aesthetic one. 'I am interested in the forms and shapes of the plants that I grow,' he tells me. 'The histories and curious life cycles fascinate me as much as the flowers they produce.' Throughout the garden there are moments where more unusual species emerge through well-loved classics, like the Leichtlin's lily (*Lilium leichtlinii*), which sits beside popular and much-admired dahlias like 'Bishop of Auckland' and 'Totally Tangerine'.

Inside, the house is a warren of sensitively restored rooms, which, thrillingly, become stages for little garden vignettes throughout the year. For Robin, there is as much pleasure to be found in creating these displays as there is in admiring their decorative quality once complete. It is an activity that he finds himself doing on a Friday evening, creating garden stories that froth from old jugs and explode from ornamental urns. 'The flowers I display in the house become like treasured objects,' Robin says. 'They are equally as important as the collected items and antiques that fill the room.'

Colour is used playfully, with the ivory walls a perfect canvas for vases overflowing with energetic red, yellow and orange flowers brought in from the garden. The flowers seem to take on greater verve in this space, as though liberated from an outside world full of distraction and allowed to shine with brilliant gusto in a gallery created just for them. The vitality and exuberance they bring to the house is not only terribly joyous but also essential to Robin. As he puts it: 'The house simply does not feel like a home until there are cut flowers positioned everywhere.'

Opposite, clockwise from top left:
A playful arrangement of chard in the kitchen; Robin's highly textured cottage garden; two stems of *Dahlia* 'Bishop of Auckland' on a mantlepiece; *Dahlia* 'Totally Tangerine' adds colour to the kitchen garden.

More is More is More...
Richard E. Grant

COLOUR PROFILE:
*Lavish yellows, royal blues and animated greens.
A bazaar of sumptuous emerald, sapphire and amethyst jewels.*

Cocooned at home among a cherished assemblage of curiosities, actor Richard E. Grant is under no doubt where he gets his energy from. 'Maximalism is my ultimate comfort and pleasure,' he tells me, and it is apparent within seconds of entering his house in southwest London that a passion for collecting antiques and interesting objects is something that pervades every part of his life.

Richard's home, a handsome Georgian house built in 1830, has quietly evolved over the thirty years he has been here. Continued layering, year after year, of items found at flea markets, auctions and trips overseas has led to rooms that are gloriously overflowing with shapes, colours and textures. Old dolls from traditional seaside puppet shows hang on the wall next to antique tapestries and gilt sconces. Pedestals and columns sit alongside elaborate side tables and daybeds. Sofas and chairs are upholstered in stripes and chintz. It is a collage, a thrilling scrapbook of decorative ideas.

The sense of fascination spreads into the garden too. A timber pavilion houses a charming collection of timeworn outdoor furniture, stage sets and statues, including a striking sculpture of Barbra Streisand's face – Richard has been a fan for more than half a century.

Opposite: A delightfully frenzied display of lady's mantle (*Alchemilla mollis*), cornflowers (*Centaurea cyanus*) and love-in-a-mist (*Nigella damascena*) on an antique bench outside Richard's sitting room window.

Opposite: An explosion of *Rosa* Boscobel ('Auscousin') adds to the assemblage of textures in the library. Above: Cornflowers (*Centaurea cyanus*), displayed on their own, bring a sense of the outdoor world to Richard's highly idiosyncratic home.

Opposite, clockwise from top left: Lady's mantle (*Alchemilla mollis*) and white love-in-a-mist (*Nigella damascena* 'Miss Jekyll Alba') displayed on a Moroccan Umberto Pasti chair in lively red; Richard's library, filled – from floor to ceiling – with decorative antiques; the garden room, which is a bazaar of outdoor curiosities; the early-19th-century house's handsome façade.

The pavilion is surrounded by a lawn with shrubs that are punctuated every now and then by a rusted bench or patinaed table.

There is an infectious energy here, an individualism that inspires a feeling of freedom and indulgence. For Richard, it represents a 'fully realized and textured way of life', and in the wonderful mix of objects that fill every inch of space, there is certainly a feeling of a life that is joyous and endlessly entertaining.

Flowers punctuate the house and only add to the energetic atmosphere. In a home full of objects, they introduce a different kind of texture and bring something of the 'other' to this indoor realm, qualities that heighten the overall dynamism and vibrancy. When a jug of garden blooms is added to a room here, it feels as though it completes an intricate and tactile tapestry.

Cut displays of flowers have the effect of framing the curiosities too. Tables, mantlepieces, shelves, cupboards and sideboards make tantalizing stage sets for flowers, dressed as they are in all manner of books, ceramics and glassware. Flowers from the garden feel at home; this indoor world resembles the wonderfully frenzied and unruly environment from which they originate in beds and borders.

There is colour in abundance. A drawing room painted in a warm ochre and a library in mint green lead to a kitchen with exposed brickwork that adds a rusticated orange to the palette. There are hundreds of book spines, creating multicoloured waves across shelving that extends the full length of a corridor connecting three rooms. Overlayed are all the dazzling hues from Richard's extensive collection of antiques and keepsakes. It is a circus of colour that in its jumbled vibrancy accepts – and indeed enhances – any colour brought in from the garden.

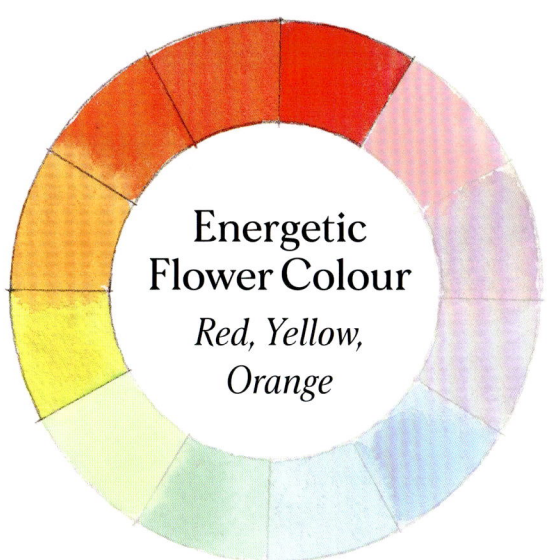

Energetic Flower Colour
Red, Yellow, Orange

Red, yellow and orange. The fiery crescendo of the colour wheel. Where delicacy and softness give way to passion and delirium. These colours excite and add instant impact, and I instinctively reach for them when I am uncertain about the kind of palette to use in a particular situation. I find myself forever seduced by their clarity and distinctiveness, and when the three are used as an analogous group, I always feel a pull towards their inherent warmth.

Energetic colours are divisive: you either love them or loathe them, especially in a garden context. For some, they epitomize the height of vulgarity, their brash colour at odds with the calm and gracefulness of the garden. For others, they represent the vitality and ambition of flowers, the thrilling climax to a season. To me, they stir the most spirited of my dreams and remind me, in days full of deadlines and meetings, that life can produce the most electrifying of surprises.

There are those who avoid loud colours simply because they are generally regarded as distasteful, but I get the sense that for some gardeners and flower arrangers they are sidestepped because they give too much away. They make too much of a statement, attract too much attention and have a suggestion of extravagance. For the more pensive and inward-looking, this can feel highly uncomfortable, but there is opportunity in this too: working with unashamedly loud and lively flower colour can become a kind of tonic. It can be a chance to explore, in a private and safe environment, aspects of a personality that might otherwise remain repressed and frustrated.

Of course, it is a mistake to stereotype red, yellow and orange as always loud and showy. For every flamboyant red dahlia (like 'Doris Day'), there is a sophisticated claret (such as 'Chat Noir'); for every sunshine-yellow tulip (like 'Flashback'), there is a delicate butter (such as 'Elegant Lady'); for every blazing orange nasturtium (like *Tropaeolum majus* 'Indian Chief'), there is a soft apricot (such as *T. minus* 'Vesuvius'). To me, even these more nuanced tones and shades have an inherent zest, an abstract feeling of liveliness and enthusiasm that is less apparent in pinks, purples, greens and blues. What they may lack in intensity, they make up for in spirit, and it is for this reason I believe they belong in schemes aiming to capture an atmosphere of energy.

Opposite: An energetic mix of dahlias and zinnias in early autumn. Blazing reds collide with sunset-oranges, syrupy marmalades and bronzed yellows to create a composition that reflects the infectious, and at times chaotic, verve of the garden at this time of year.

Red

Red is full of contradiction. In one sense, it is a warning – the universal colour of danger – and in another it is pure passion and seduction. It is loud and fiery and then dark and brooding. Where in some cases it is the embodiment of unabashed excitement, in others it is the dull thud of pain. A primary colour, one certain aspect of red is that it is always decisive and never short of energy.

In the garden, red's complementary colour, ubiquitous green, ensures that it always commands attention; as opposites on the colour wheel, the two hues have a natural and intrinsic partnership that draws the best out of the other. Like strawberries and cream, macaroni and cheese, or gin and tonic, red and green come together to create something greater than their constituent parts, and there is therefore perhaps no better place than a garden, so consumed with green, to apply red to most striking effect.

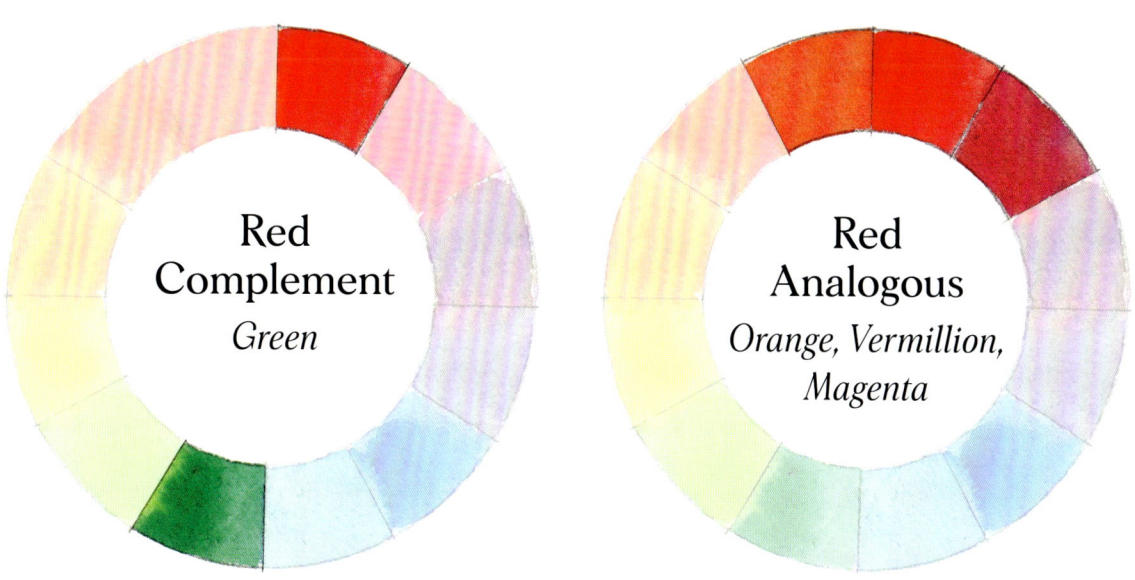

Opposite: Red scrapbook. A journey through the garden year that is as passionate and sultry as it is surprising and unpredictable.

ATMOSPHERE 2: ENERGETIC

Plant Profiles: Blazing Red

Untamed passion. Fiery, tumultuous and unpredictable. Colours that assert control.

Dahlia 'Bishop of Auckland'

Perennial • Late summer to autumn • Height: up to 1m (39in), spread: up to 1m (39in) • Full sun • All soil types • Vase life: excellent (1+ week) • Flower colour value: mid-to-dark

The 'Bishop' dahlias have long been firm favourites, seen by many as a more sophisticated alternative to the brashness of most cultivars. Where others dazzle with double flowers and petals that contort into intricate geometric patterns, the 'Bishops' are largely simple, single blooms. 'Bishop of Auckland' is a deep, seductive red. There is an undercurrent of dark purple through the petals – a hidden depth that adds mystery – and, at the flower's centre, a wheel of stamens brilliantly contrasts in sparkling yellow. This is a vibrant dahlia, but, unlike others, its exuberance is contained and the colour never seems too overpowering. Instead, it is a red I long for and I feel regret when the last flower is cut for the house.

Planting note: This 'Bishop' works as part of a prairie planting and looks particularly effective with ornamental grasses – *Pennisetum advena* 'Rubrum' is an excellent analogous choice.

In-season complementary colour: *Echinacea purpurea* 'Green Jewel' (chartreuse), *Moluccella laevis* (mid-green), *Zinnia elegans* 'Envy' (chartreuse)

In-season analogous colour: *Bistorta amplexicaulis* 'Fat Domino' (raspberry), *Rudbeckia hirta* 'Autumn Colours' (rust-red), *Tithonia rotundifolia* 'Torch' (mid-orange)

Lathyrus odoratus 'Winston Churchill' (sweet pea)

Annual • Summer • Height: up to 1.8m (6ft), spread: up to 50cm (20in) • Full sun • All soil types except very heavy clay • Vase life: good (up to 1 week) • Flower colour value: mid-to-dark

'Winston Churchill' is a sweet pea cultivar with a certain *joie de vivre*. A glossy and sprightly red that is infused with electric orange and then deepened by cherry, it feels so appropriately vivacious for a time of year teeming with new life. As with all sweet peas, its petals are gloriously ruffled and make for exquisite cut flowers, and the more you cut, the more it blooms. The delightful scent of 'Winston Churchill' alone should be reason enough to bring bucketfuls indoors, but if that is not persuasive enough, its colour ought to be the deciding factor. It glistens and reflects the light when placed by a window, bathing the room in its sparkling energy.

Planting note: 'Winston Churchill' looks attractive growing up wigwams or trellises in loose cottage garden schemes. Continuous cutting prolongs flowering.

In-season complementary colour: *Alchemilla mollis* (chartreuse), *Allium obliquum* (chartreuse), *Euphorbia amygdaloides* var. *robbiae* (chartreuse)

In-season analogous colour: *Cosmos atrosanguineus* Cherry Chocolate (cerise), *Oenothera lindheimeri* Geyser Pink ('Gaudros') (cerise), *Rosa* Thomas à Becket ('Auswinston') (ruby)

Tagetes patula 'Burning Embers' (French marigold)

Annual • Summer to autumn • Height: up to 50cm (20in), spread: up to 50cm (20in) • Full sun • All soil types • Vase life: excellent (1+ week) • Flower colour value: mid-to-dark

One of my all-time favourite annuals, *Tagetes patula* 'Burning Embers' is best known as a companion plant to tomatoes – where it is sown to protect against aphids and whitefly – but in its own right it produces the most handsome little flowers. It develops quickly into a bushy plant that supports long, protruding stems with masses of coin-shaped blooms. The tiny petals are each edged with a border of canary yellow before becoming inflamed in a curiously ambiguous kind of red. It is bright but also somehow deep and smouldering, appearing in some lights to lean towards orange, but in others more towards brown. The underside of the petals is a glorious mustard.

Planting note: This is a fast-growing plant that flowers within a few weeks of sowing, which makes it incredibly useful for filling gaps that emerge unexpectedly throughout the season.

In-season complementary colour: *Echinacea purpurea* 'Green Jewel' (chartreuse), *Moluccella laevis* (mid-green), *Zinnia elegans* 'Envy' (chartreuse)

In-season analogous colour: *Cosmos bipinnatus* 'Rubenza' (ruby), *Echinacea* SunSeekers Red (mid-red), *Tropaeolum majus* 'Red Troika' (mid-red)

Tulipa 'Couleur Cardinal'

Perennial bulb (often treated as an annual) • Spring • Height: up to 30cm (12in), spread: up to 10cm (4in) • Full sun to partial shade • All soil types except very heavy clay • Vase life: excellent (1+ week) • Flower colour value: mid-to-dark

I think red is rather rare in the spring garden, a time that seems dominated by the cool blues and cheery yellows of early bulbs like grape hyacinths (*Muscari*), *Crocus* and *Narcissus*. The reds that reign over the crescendo of summer and the embers of autumn seem far away. Tulips, however, allow for an early shot of red's vitality, and none are more splendid than 'Couleur Cardinal'. This ancient variety with single, cupped flowers has long beguiled gardeners with its colouring. At first, the flower appears to be an all-over ruby, but closer observation reveals influences of violet on the outer petals and yellow within.

Planting note: This tulip does not have the longest of stems, making it ideal as part of an understorey for taller cultivars in similarly energetic tones – 'Carnaval de Rio', 'El Niño' and 'Red Impression' work well.

In-season complementary colour: *Euphorbia amygdaloides* var. *robbiae* (chartreuse), *Euphorbia epithymoides* (chartreuse), *Helleborus viridis* (chartreuse)

In-season analogous colour: *Anemone coronaria* 'Hollandia' (mid-red), *Erysimum cheiri* 'Sugar Rush Red' (ruby), *Tiarella* 'Pink Skyrocket' (salmon)

Plant Profiles: Sophisticated Red

Alluring and refined, this is red at its most mature.
A polished energy that is elegant and gracious in its vivacity.

Centranthus ruber 'Roseus' (red valerian)

Perennial • Summer • Height: up to 1m (39in), spread: up to 50cm (20in) • Full sun to partial shade • All soil types except very heavy clay • Vase life: good (up to 1 week) • Flower colour value: mid

Where I live in Somerset, red valerian grows everywhere. In summer, it peppers hedgerows, emerges from stone walls and edges the little lanes that meander through the hills. It is often overlooked as an ornamental garden plant. However, I cannot think of a more perfect red than 'Roseus'. It is a colour with tremendous sophistication and complexity, a scarlet that leans towards pink but has undercurrents of deep merlot. As the flowers cascade down long stems in a complementary mid-green, they appear like celebratory fireworks fizzing above the surrounding planting.

Planting note: 'Roseus' benefits from continuous cutting back throughout the season to prolong flowering. This is a plant that, in favourable conditions, will freely self-seed, so some maintenance is required if the aim is to curtail its spread across the garden.

In-season complementary colour: *Alchemilla mollis* (chartreuse), *Euphorbia amygdaloides* var. *robbiae* (chartreuse), *Euphorbia epithymoides* (chartreuse)

In-season analogous colour: *Allium hollandicum* 'Purple Sensation' (mid-purple), *Astilbe* 'Rheinland' (powder pink), *Rosa* 'Albertine' (salmon)

Cosmos atrosanguineus Cherry Chocolate

Perennial • Summer to autumn • Height: up to 50cm (20in), spread: up to 50cm (20in) • Full sun • All soil types • Vase life: good (up to 1 week) • Flower colour value: mid-to-dark

Cosmos of all kinds are, as far as I am concerned, one of the underrated stars of any garden. There is one cultivar, however, that I think stands head and shoulders above the others in terms of depth and complexity of colour: Cherry Chocolate. A gloriously elegant flower, its petals are an impossibly rich ruby, the colour of an earthy red wine. It is a red that changes throughout the day as light moves across the garden: at dawn and dusk, the flowers have a darker, brooding quality, yet under the spotlight of midday sun, they transform into a glistening cerise. Unlike other cosmos, this is a hardy, perennial variety.

Planting note: Cherry Chocolate is relatively compact and produces flowers on shorter stems than other types of cosmos, which makes it perfect for growing in a container. Every year there are always one or two pots of them in my garden, usually mixed with gaura (*Oenothera lindheimeri*).

In-season complementary colour: *Echinacea purpurea* 'Green Jewel' (chartreuse), *Nicotiana langsdorffii* (chartreuse), *Zinnia elegans* 'Envy' (chartreuse)

In-season analogous colour: *Dahlia* 'Arabian Night' (merlot), *Dahlia* 'Mexican Star' (chocolate), *Salvia* 'Royal Bumble' (mid-red)

Dahlia 'Arabian Night'

Perennial • Late summer to autumn • Height: up to 1m (39in), spread: up to 1m (39in) • Full sun • All soil types • Vase life: excellent (1+ week) • Flower colour value: dark

There is a mystery to 'Arabian Night', a vacillating quality that bounces between moody introspection and lively effervescence. In dull light, its flowers wear a cloak of darkness; they appear shadowy and murky, as though waiting in the wings ready to emerge into a spotlight that reveals their true splendour. When that light comes, the flowers transform into an extraordinary deep red that is full of energy, but also discerning and refined. It is the colour of Pinot Noir, an irresistible cherry that feels mature and discriminating. As with all dahlias, 'Arabian Night' flowers intensely as summer turns to autumn, and at this time its enigmatic colour brings a sophisticated end to the growing season.

Planting note: 'Arabian Night' looks attractive as part of a mixed dahlia border where brighter varieties play off its darker temperament. Varieties such as 'Ambition', 'Bishop of York' and 'Golden Scepter' make attractive neighbours.

In-season complementary colour: *Echinacea purpurea* 'Green Jewel' (chartreuse), *Moluccella laevis* (mid-green), *Zinnia elegans* 'Envy' (chartreuse)

In-season analogous colour: *Anemone* × *hybrida* 'September Charm' (powder pink), *Symphyotrichum novae-angliae* 'Harrington's Pink' (candy pink), *Verbena bonariensis* (mid-purple)

Dianthus barbatus 'Electron Mix' (sweet William)

Biennial or short-lived perennial • Summer • Height: up to 50cm (20in), spread: up to 50cm (20in) • Full sun • All soil types • Vase life: excellent (1+ week) • Flower colour value: mid-to-dark

Dianthus has unfairly, if you ask me, suffered from the fickle whims of fashion and is all too often disregarded as old hat. It is unlikely ever again to be the most stylish or sought-after plant in the summer garden, but that should not stop its energetic performance from being admired. The 'Electron Mix' is a particular favourite for the wonderful, raspberry-red flowers produced in huge masses over a long period from the end of spring. Sturdy stems support mopheads of flowers, with each petal displaying an intricately woven pattern of colour. The flowers create a Persian carpet of jewel-like tones and shades that shimmer in the brilliant light of mid-summer.

Planting note: *Dianthus* are mostly biennial – sown one year to flower and die back the next – but the 'Electron Mix' tends to behave like a perennial (albeit short-lived).

In-season complementary colour: *Alchemilla mollis* (chartreuse), *Allium obliquum* (chartreuse), *Euphorbia amygdaloides* var. *robbiae* (chartreuse)

In-season analogous colour: *Geum* 'Mrs J. Bradshaw' (vermillion), *Lathyrus odoratus* 'King Edward VII' (mid-red), *Papaver rhoeas* (mid-red)

Yellow

Perhaps the most divisive colour of them all, yellow is a primary that, love or loathe it, has an unstoppable energy. It is a hue often seen as immature – the reserve of children's toys and colouring books – which does the complexity of its tones and shades a disservice. When we begin to explore the sensory world around us as babies, we are drawn to the brightest, most conspicuous of stimuli, and as the brightest of any colour, we therefore gravitate towards yellow with enthusiasm. It seems that as adults we remember yellow's juvenile magnetism and in turn consider it no longer sophisticated enough for our more refined sensibility. But what if we embraced yellow and celebrated its naivety: perhaps we would find that there is joy in relinquishing the shackles of good taste?

Yellow in the garden is, to me, a breath of fresh air. It sparkles and glistens with positivity, a colour that uplifts and motivates. I perhaps associate it most with the optimism and rebirth of spring. At this time there are drifts of daffodils and crocuses in sunshine-lemons together with primroses and cowslips in a more restrained butter-yellow. These are flowers that excite me, and the opportunity to bring their cheerful colour into the house is something I relish as a new growing season begins.

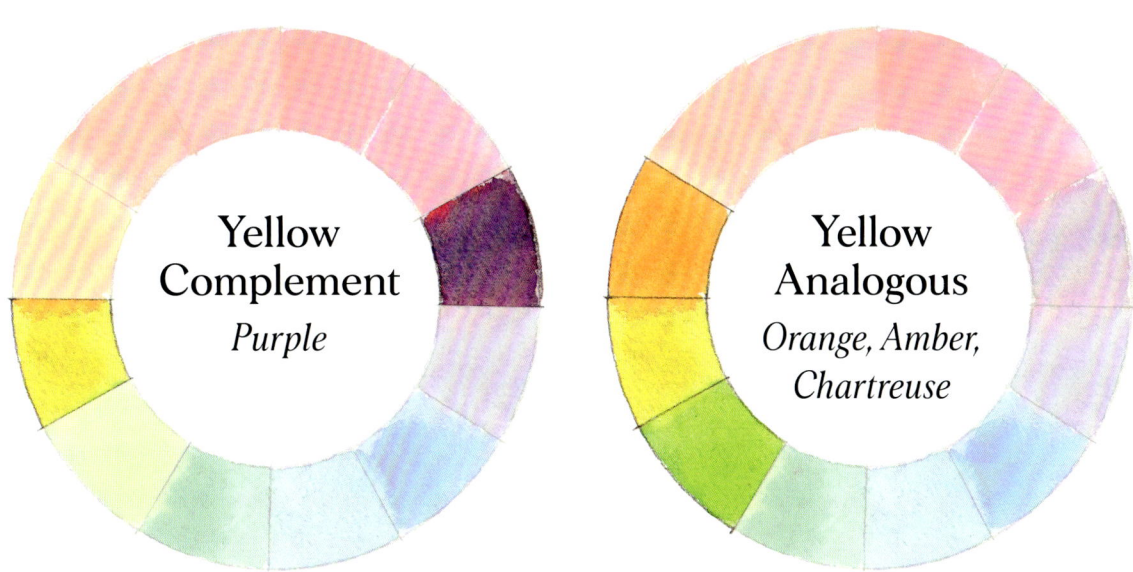

Opposite: Yellow scrapbook. The most contentious colour of them all, yellow is, to me, one of the garden's greatest joys.

ATMOSPHERE 2: ENERGETIC

Plant Profiles: Brilliant Yellow

Freedom. The boundless energy of youth. The kind of laughter where for a moment everything else is forgotten. Colour at its most liberated.

Aquilegia chrysantha 'Yellow Queen' (columbine)

Perennial • Late spring • Height: up to 1m (39in), spread: up to 50cm (20in) • Full sun to partial shade • All soil types except very heavy clay • Vase life: excellent (1+ week) • Flower colour value: light

A serious contender for my favourite flower (although this is subject to change on a daily basis), *Aquilegia chrysantha* 'Yellow Queen', with its wonderfully exaggerated flowers, is a highlight of the late spring garden. Petals are tight and cup-shaped at the centre, but looser and more informal on the outside, with elongated spurs soaring from the rear. They tower above clumps of mid-green foliage, their heads bobbing in the slightest wind. Yet it is their colour that I find most extraordinary. The centre of the flower is a saturated lemon – bright and utterly joyous – before moving to a more buttery tone as the petals become untethered. In groups they create an electrifying yellow display that feels pure and uncomplicated.

Planting note: Try in a container of early summer planting. Ferns, foxgloves and alliums make for attractive companions.

In-season complementary colour: *Allium hollandicum* 'Purple Sensation' (mid-purple), *Iris germanica* 'Emma Louise' (mauve-violet), *Iris germanica* 'Lent A. Williamson' (mauve-purple)

In-season analogous colour: *Alchemilla mollis* (chartreuse), *Rosa* Lady of Shalott ('Ausnyson') (apricot), *Rosa* Port Sunlight ('Auslofty') (apricot)

Dahlia 'Bishop of York'

Perennial • Late summer to autumn • Height: up to 1m (39in), spread: up to 1m (39in) • Full sun • All soil types • Vase life: excellent (1+ week) • Flower colour value: light

There is no shortage of bright dahlias to choose from, but one that I think manages to have a sense of exuberance, while also offering a certain level of sophistication, is 'Bishop of York'. Simple, single flowers are washed in a delightful cadmium-yellow, which, depending on the clarity of light, feels either close to mustard or close to canary. Either way, the flowers pop excitedly against the dark chocolate of the stems and foliage. On some petals there can be a subtle dusting of peach, which adds an attractive layer of complexity.

Planting note: 'Bishop of York' looks attractive emerging towards the front of a mixed dahlia border. It brings a level of refinement when grouped with varieties in analogous colours (such as 'Kelvin Floodlight', 'Golden Scepter' and 'Sylvia').

In-season complementary colour: *Salvia nemorosa* 'Caradonna' (violet-purple), *Scabiosa atropurpurea* 'Black Knight' (dark purple), *Verbena bonariensis* (mid-purple)

In-season analogous colour: *Crocosmia × crocosmiiflora* 'Emily Mckenzie' (mid-orange), *Helenium* 'Rubinzwerg' (vermillion), *Helianthus annuus* 'Velvet Queen' (deep copper)

Epimedium × *versicolor* 'Sulphureum'

Perennial • Spring • Height: up to 50cm (20in), spread: up to 50cm (20in) • Full sun to full shade • All soil types except very heavy clay • Vase life: good (up to 1 week) • Flower colour value: light

Epimediums are invaluable plants for adding interest to difficult areas of shade, and with many varieties being evergreen, it is their ground-cover foliage that is most highly prized for much of the year. 'Sulphureum' is no exception, with rusted, heart-shaped leaves forming dense mounds that look very attractive when used as underplanting for trees and shrubs. While the foliage is undoubtedly a huge plus, it is, however, the delightfully small flowers that most inspire me. Emerging on tiny, bronzed stems, the blooms consist of a central citrus cup that is surrounded by a halo of creamy petals. The flowers cascade informally to produce a rather frenzied and haphazard performance, which only adds to their charm.

Planting note: 'Sulphureum' looks most charming in drifts as underplanting for trees and shrubs. It combines well in spring with daffodils in analogous shades to create a spectacle of yellow.

In-season complementary colour: *Lunaria annua* (mauve), *Tulipa* 'Merlot' (merlot), *Tulipa* 'Queen of Night' (dark purple)

In-season analogous colour: *Narcissus* 'Eaton Song' (mid-yellow), *Narcissus* 'Replete' (white with peach), *Narcissus* 'Tahiti' (butter-yellow)

Viola × *wittrockiana* 'Frizzle Sizzle Yellow-blue Swirl' (pansy)

Annual • Autumn to spring • Height: 20cm (8in), spread: 20cm (8in) • Full sun to partial shade • All soil types • Vase life: good (up to 1 week) • Flower colour value: light-to-mid

How could anyone not fall for a flower called 'Frizzle Sizzle Yellow-blue Swirl'? This is a wonderfully eccentric pansy which flowers for an extraordinarily long period from autumn to spring. Lower petals glow in an electric canary yellow, which fades to a pale lemon at the edges, dark brown stripes racing across their surface. Upper petals are less saturated – they appear more like a creamy butter – but are then infused at the sides with complementary violet. It really is the most cheering sight over winter.

Planting note: This pansy looks attractive in shallow containers. I usually have one or two terracotta bowls planted with them, which I make sure I can see from the window over the winter.

In-season complementary colour: *Fritillaria meleagris* (mid-purple), *Hyacinthus orientalis* 'Purple Sensation' (mid-purple), *Iris reticulata* 'J.S. Dijt' (mid-purple)

In-season analogous colour: *Narcissus* 'February Gold' (mid-yellow), *Narcissus* 'Moonlight Sensation' (butter-yellow), *Narcissus* 'My Story' (white with peach)

Plant Profiles: Butter-Yellow

Creamy, soft and translucent. Velvety butter-yellow of whisked cake batter. The colour of freshly squeezed lemon juice. Polite and well-mannered yellow.

Cosmos bipinnatus 'Xanthos'

Annual • Summer to autumn • Height: 60cm (24in), spread: 30cm (12in) • Full sun • All soil types • Vase life: good (up to 1 week) • Flower colour value: light

'Xanthos' has a pleasant cooling effect on the summer garden, like ice placed in a cold drink on a blisteringly hot afternoon. Where everything else is ablaze in the brightest pinks, reds and oranges, this cosmos shimmers in a delightful lemonade. The petals are a kind of clotted cream and palest where they meet a disc of sunshine-yellow stamens at the base. Towards the tips the petals are more saturated with a velvety butterscotch that has the slightest hint of baby pink. The flowers are suspended above emerald-green, dissected foliage, so they appear to dance like ballerinas in frilly tutus in the wind.

Planting note: As an annual, 'Xanthos' is effective in quickly covering gaps in beds and borders or replacing interest that died back earlier in the season. I am often tempted to plant it alongside once-flowering roses, so the abundant flowers can extend the performance in that area once the roses have finished flowering.

In-season complementary colour: *Lathyrus odoratus* 'Blue Velvet' (deep purple), *Penstemon* 'Raven' (mid-purple), *Rosa* Munstead Wood ('Ausbernard') (merlot)

In-season analogous colour: *Calendula officinalis* 'Indian Prince' (mid-orange), *Dahlia* 'Catherine Deneuve' (apricot), *Tropaeolum majus* 'Tom Thumb' (mid-orange)

Narcissus bulbocodium 'Arctic Bells' (daffodil)

Perennial bulb • Spring • Height: 20cm (8in), spread: 20cm (8in) • Full sun to partial shade • All soil types • Vase life: excellent (1+ week) • Flower colour value: light

'Arctic Bells' is a Bulbocodium daffodil. With large coronas that overshadow the surrounding petals, this is a distinctive cultivar with quite a different feel to the more traditional and recognizable daffodil form. Hoop petticoat daffodils, as *Narcissus bulbocodium* are called, are highly attractive little flowers, and their short stature makes them perfect for small containers. 'Arctic Bells' is the colour of butter as it melts on warm toast, a soft and pearly kind of yellow. There is the hint of something more exuberant inside the corona, but, overall, these demure flowers wear their colour with modesty.

Planting note: In the ground there is a risk that 'Arctic Bells' will become lost and overshadowed by the emerging foliage of summer perennials. However, in small pots, they look delightful as part of a group of containers, all planted individually with different daffodil varieties.

In-season complementary colour : *Fritillaria meleagris* (mid-purple), *Hyacinthus orientalis* 'Purple Sensation' (mid-purple), *Iris reticulata* 'J.S. Dijt' (mid-purple)

In-season analogous colour: *Epimedium × versicolor* 'Sulphureum' (lemon-yellow), *Erysimum* 'Apricot Delight' (apricot), *Erysimum* 'Constant Cheer' (apricot to pink-purple)

Rosa 'Emily Gray'

Perennial, rambling rose • Early summer (once-flowering) • Height: up to 8m (26ft), spread: up to 4m (13ft) • Full sun to partial shade • Vase life: good (up to 1 week) • Flower colour value: light-to-mid

'Emily Gray' is a vigorous rambling rose that flowers prolifically in early summer. Its blooms are ruffled and semi-double, with petals that are informally arranged around a central, sunken ring of stamens. It is the colour of pure butterscotch, a creamy and indulgent kind of yellow that feels as though it should be topping a cake. The flowers are surrounded by glossy, forest-green foliage, which accentuates their luxuriousness. 'Emily Gray' is a favourite for cutting and mixing with other roses in a jug for the house. Its vase life is shorter than that of other varieties, but this does not stop me enjoying it inside the cottage for a day or two.

Planting note: 'Emily Gray' requires sturdy support in order to reach its full potential. It can be a good idea to grow a clematis or jasmine through the rose to extend interest after it finishes flowering in early summer.

In-season complementary colour: *Geranium phaeum* 'Raven' (mid-purple), *Lathyrus odoratus* 'Blue Velvet' (deep purple), *Nepeta racemosa* 'Walker's Low' (violet-blue)

In-season analogous colour: *Iris germanica* 'Benton Apollo' (lemon-yellow), *Iris germanica* 'Saint Crispin' (mid-yellow), *Phlomis russeliana* (lemon-butter)

Tulipa turkestanica (Turkestan tulip)

Perennial bulb • Spring • Height: 30cm (12in), spread: 10cm (4in) • Full sun to partial shade • Vase life: good (up to 1 week) • Flower colour value: light

Tulips are perhaps best known for the showy and flamboyant chorus of colour they bring to the spring garden. And while I certainly admire them for this, there are tulips that are altogether more genteel. *Tulipa turkestanica*, a species tulip, is a good example. Where most hybrid cultivars are tall, dramatic and feverishly pigmented, this is a small plant with delicate colouring. Held on impossibly slender stems, its blooms open into a perfect star shape when the sun shines, and while much of the petals are a buttermilk-white, there is a bewitching moment at the base where a splash of egg-yolk-yellow appears. Fragile, tender and reticent, *T. turkestanica* has a completely different feel to its hybridized cousins, but is in no way any less captivating.

Planting note: Unlike hybridized tulips, *Tulipa turkestanica* is fully perennial and will, over time, naturalize in the garden to create attractive drifts of soft spring colour.

In-season complementary colour: *Crocus tommasinianus* 'Barr's Purple' (mid-purple), *Iris reticulata* 'Purple Hill' (magenta-purple), *Tulipa* 'Magic Lavender' (lilac)

In-season analogous colour: *Erysimum* 'Golden Jubilee' (butter-yellow), *Erysimum* Walberton's Fragrant Sunshine (mid-yellow), *Narcissus* 'Hawera' (mid-yellow)

Orange

Underneath orange's vitality there is a slight sense of mystery. As a secondary colour, formed from the blending of two primaries, it is a hue that is pulled in opposing directions: the certainty and assertiveness of red against the naivety and pluckiness of yellow. The result means it is not always obvious how we should read its intentions – is it warm and friendly or is it burning and hostile?

I am under no doubt that orange flowers are among the very best; they have an unmatched honesty, a charm in their brashness. While it is impossible not to feel uplifted by the brightest tones – the blazing sunsets of rudbeckia, the splashy effervescence of nasturtiums – this is a colour with an immense capacity for nuance. There are endless cultivars of peaches, apricots and marmalades, softer tones that restrain orange's full capacity for shock and awe, but take nothing away from its energetic spirit.

Blue is its complement, but as with yellow and purple, it is perhaps not the first partnership towards which many gardeners or flower arrangers would gravitate when planting a border or filling a vase. In fact, I would probably go as far as to say that for most this pairing would be regarded as highly distasteful. It is difficult because the two colours represent two opposing ideas: where orange is warm; blue is cool. There is a tension in their coupling that the eye struggles to resolve; it is night versus day, a summer afternoon versus a winter frost.

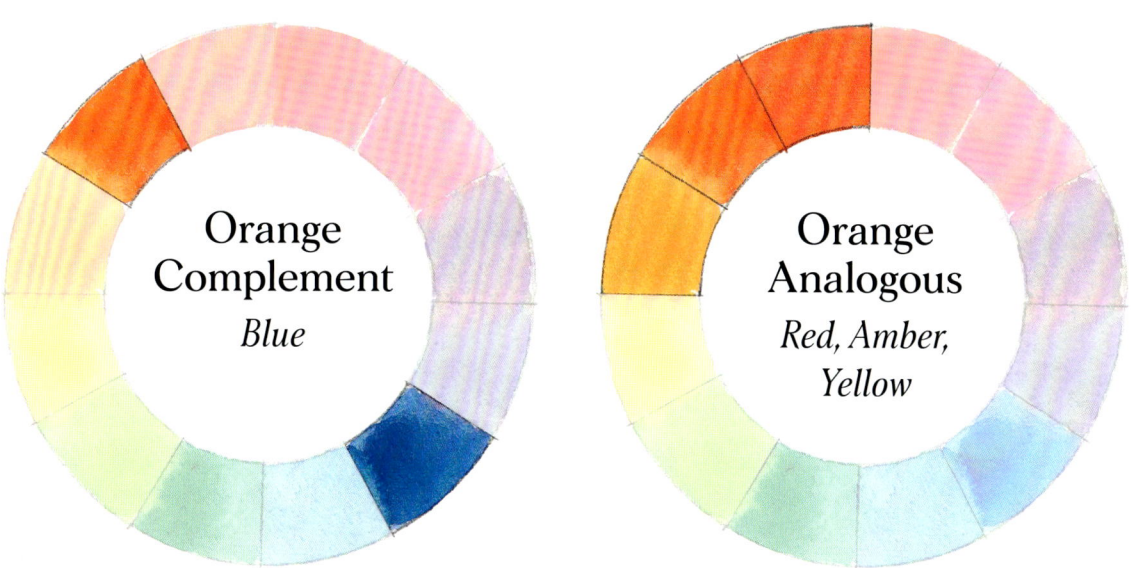

Opposite: Orange scrapbook. Warming, gregarious and uncompromising, the orange garden is planting at its most flamboyant.

Plant Profiles: Classy Orange

Apricot jam, the dying moments of a summer sunset, an autumn woodland gently rusting. Sensitive and discerning orange. Orange on its best behaviour.

Iris germanica 'Grand Chief' (bearded iris)

Perennial • Late spring • Height: up to 1m (39in), spread: up to 50cm (20in) • Full sun • All soil types • Vase life: good (up to 1 week) • Flower colour value: mid

'Grand Chief' is a curious bearded iris in the spring garden in that its colouring feels more akin to autumn. With dusty amber standards sitting on top of rusted falls, it resembles a golden woodland in the dying moments of a harvest sunset and would feel at home among fiery dahlias and bronzed sunflowers (*Helianthus*). The dark falls are lightly veined towards the throat and contrast strikingly with a lemony beard. Its smouldering appearance is a welcome distraction from the sweetness of early summer.

Planting note: 'Grand Chief' looks attractive planted in drifts through emerging summer perennials. After flowering, its upright foliage remains and adds textural value to a planting composition.

In-season complementary colour: *Hyacinthoides non-scripta* (mid-blue), *Myosotis sylvatica* (sky-blue), *Nigella damascena* 'Miss Jekyll' (sky-blue)

In-season analogous colour: *Digitalis × valinii* 'Firecracker' (apricot), *Rosa* Port Sunlight ('Auslofty') (apricot), *Rosa* Thomas à Becket ('Auswinston') (ruby)

Lilium Tiger Babies Group (lily)

Perennial • Summer • Height: up to 1.5m (5ft), spread: up to 50cm (20in) • Full sun to partial shade • All soil types • Vase life: excellent (1+ week) • Flower colour value: light-to-mid

There is something so incredibly joyous and uncomplicated about lilies. They are rarely thought of as the most fashionable or sought-after flowers in a garden, but to me they have a timeless charm that transcends the comings and goings of planting trends. There is a playfulness to them, a sense of high summer frivolity as they bounce through beds and borders. Tiger Babies Group is a particularly captivating cultivar that flowers in a sophisticated peach, its recurved petals each blotted with dashes of dark cherry.

Planting note: This cultivar looks attractive emerging through neutral grasses or textural perennials like lady's mantle (*Alchemilla mollis*) and Baltic parsley (*Cenolophium denudatum*).

In-season complementary colour: *Centaurea cyanus* (mid-blue), *Delphinium* Black Knight Group (mid-blue), *Nigella damascena* 'Miss Jekyll' (sky-blue)

In-season analogous colour: *Eschscholzia californica* 'Orange King' (mid-orange), *Lathyrus odoratus* 'Prince of Orange' (coral), *Tropaeolum majus* 'Tom Thumb' (mid-orange)

Rosa Lady of Shalott ('Ausnyson')

Perennial, English shrub rose • Summer to autumn (repeat-flowering) • Height: up to 1.5m (5ft), spread: up to 1m (39in) • Full sun to partial shade • All soil types • Vase life: good (up to 1 week) • Flower colour value: mid

Roses are, to me, the ultimate romantic flower, appearing most often in my garden or as part of indoor cut displays in a melee of pinks. However, there are a handful of cultivars that I adore for their more energetic and zestful colour, of which *Rosa* Lady of Shalott is a firm favourite. A sprawling shrub growing to around 1.5m (5ft) in height, this is a rose that dazzles in a fruity cocktail of orange. At the flower's centre, the petals are flushed with deep sunset-apricot, but as they begin to unfurl, they become lighter and tinged with a touch of coral at the edges. It is a flower that manages to appear both exuberant and graceful, a glorious enigma in the summer garden.

Planting note: *Rosa* Lady of Shalott is a striking rose that commands attention. Anything more subtle is likely to be lost in its wake, so it is a good idea to group with more exuberant planting where a true spectacle of colour can be enjoyed.

In-season complementary colour: *Agapanthus* Brilliant Blue (mid-blue), *Delphinium* Black Knight Group (mid-blue), *Geranium* Rozanne (blue-mauve)

In-season analogous colour: *Calendula officinalis* 'Indian Prince' (mid-orange), *Digitalis × valinii* 'Firecracker' (apricot), *Lupinus* Terracotta (apricot)

Rudbeckia hirta 'Autumn Colours'

Perennial • Late summer • Height: up to 50cm (20in), spread: up to 50cm (20in) • Full sun to partial shade • Clay and loam soil types • Vase life: excellent (1+ week) • Flower colour value: mid-to-dark

Rudbeckias are invaluable perennials, firing the garden into the final throws of the growing season. Their loose, floriferous habit ensures the garden retains a sense of abundance as most perennials begin to fade. 'Autumn Colours' encapsulates the blazing spirit of this time of year. The large, daisy-like flowers have slender petals radiating from a tawny centre. Each petal fades from a dusty tangerine at the tip to bronze at the base, which, since the petals are arranged in a perfect fan, creates an illusion of colour in concentric rings. This flower feels antique, as if it has sat in the garden for decades and slowly weathered.

Planting note: 'Autumn Colours' is short compared with other rudbeckias and is best placed at the front of a scheme. Its fiery colouring looks good with perennials in analogous tones and shades, such as crocosmias (try 'Emily McKenzie' or 'Hellfire') and heleniums (try 'Moerheim Beauty' or 'Waltraut').

In-season complementary colour: *Aster × frikartii* 'Mönch' (blue-mauve), *Salvia* 'Blue Butterflies' (mid-blue), *Salvia uliginosa* (sky-blue)

In-season analogous colour: *Crocosmia* 'Hellfire' (vermillion), *Dahlia* 'David Howard' (apricot), *Dahlia* 'Cornel Brons' (apricot)

Plant Profiles: Splashy Orange

A carnival parade. The pure, undiluted joy of life. The kind of orange that transports you to a Sicilian citrus grove. Orange that fizzes with abandon.

Crocosmia × *crocosmiiflora* 'Emily McKenzie' (montbretia)

Perennial • Late summer • Height: up to 1m (39in), spread: up to 50cm (20in) • Full sun to partial shade • All soil types • Vase life: excellent (1+ week) • Flower colour value: light-to-mid

Crocosmia can be overlooked in late summer in the frenzy of dahlias, heleniums, rudbeckias and later annuals. The flowers may not be as showy, but they do match the energy of these plants, and, in many ways, in a more elegant manner. With its layers of colour, 'Emily McKenzie' is perhaps my favourite. Mid-green foliage appears from late spring and has a grass-like quality that adds texture to a mixed bed or border. As summer progresses, arching stems launch from the leaves, which go on to support the star-shaped flowers in brilliant orange. It is an electrifying colour: bright and buoyant. The petals surround a yellow throat, each one brushed at the base with mahogany.

Planting note: 'Emily McKenzie' looks attractive emerging through grasses or with late summer perennials in similarly fiery colours. Try with heleniums ('Moerheim Beauty' and 'Waltraut') or rudbeckias ('Autumn Colours' and 'Goldsturm').

In-season complementary colour: *Agapanthus campanulatus* 'Cobalt Blue' (mid-blue), *Echinops bannaticus* 'Taplow Blue' (powder blue), *Salvia guaranitica* 'Black and Blue' (mid-blue)

In-season analogous colour: *Calendula officinalis* 'Indian Prince' (mid-orange), *Dahlia* 'Cornel Brons' (apricot), *Tropaeolum majus* Jewel of Africa Group (mid-orange)

Tithonia rotundifolia 'Torch' (Mexican sunflower)

Annual • Summer • Height: up to 1.8m (6ft), spread: up to 30cm (12in) • Full sun • All soil types except very heavy clay • Vase life: good (up to 1 week) • Flower colour value: mid

Tithonia is not as widely grown as other annuals, which is a shame because one of its many attributes is the energetic pop of colour it brings to the late summer garden. 'Torch' grows into a bushy plant that can reach 1.8m (6ft), making it invaluable for adding height to gaps in beds and borders. The flowers are relatively simple in appearance – similar, as their common name suggests, to a sunflower – but their colour is exceptional. Orange petals surround a central disc of amber stamens; this orange feels buoyed by copious amounts of lemon and yet, at the same time, nuanced by a hint of claret.

Planting note: The height of this makes it valuable at the back of beds and borders in late summer. It looks attractive mixed with dahlias of equal stature in analogous colours. Cultivars such as 'David Howard', 'Ludwig Helfert', 'Golden Scepter' and 'Bishop of Llandaff' make interesting neighbours.

In-season complementary colour: *Aster* × *frikartii* 'Mönch' (blue-mauve), *Echinops bannaticus* 'Taplow Blue' (powder blue), *Salvia uliginosa* (sky-blue)

In-season analogous colour: *Calendula officinalis* 'Calexis Yellow' (mid-yellow), *Dahlia* 'Catherine Deneuve' (apricot), *Tropaeolum majus* 'Tom Thumb' (mid-orange)

Tropaeolum majus Jewel of Africa Group (nasturtium)

Annual • Summer • Height: up to 2.4m (8ft), spread: up to 1.5m (5ft) • Full sun • All soil types (flowering improves in poor soil) • Vase life: excellent (1+ week) • Flower colour value: mid

Nasturtiums are nostalgic plants that instantly soften a garden with their carefree informality. Although there are cultivars in yellows and reds, the colour for which they are best known is orange. This *Tropaeolum* is a good climber with suitable support, blanketing a trellis or wigwam in wonderfully marbled foliage. Buds burst open into trumpet-shaped flowers in deep saffron (the Jewel of Africa Group produces red and yellow flowers too). This is flora at its most uninhibited; an explosion of orange that reminds you how unpredictable nature can be. What they lack in sophistication, nasturtiums make up for in spirited endeavour.

Planting note: Traditionally grown in the kitchen garden, nasturtiums also deserve a place in main beds and borders. Low-growing cultivars like 'Tom Thumb' are excellent at the front of a scheme, whereas the Jewel of Africa Group looks wonderful racing up a wigwam among summer perennials.

In-season complementary colour: *Agapanthus campanulatus* 'Cobalt Blue' (mid-blue), *Nigella damascena* 'Miss Jekyll' (sky-blue), *Salvia guaranitica* 'Black and Blue' (mid-blue)

In-season analogous colour: *Calendula officinalis* 'Indian Prince' (mid-orange), *Dahlia* 'Cornel Brons' (apricot), *Dahlia* 'David Howard' (apricot)

Tulipa 'Ballerina'

Perennial bulb (often treated as an annual) • Spring • Height: up to 60cm (24in), spread: up to 15cm (6in) • Full sun to partial shade • All soil types except very heavy clay • Vase life: excellent (1+ week) • Flower colour value: light-to-mid

'Ballerina' is in the Lily-flowered Group, having slender and elegantly flared petals. As its name suggests, it brings a gracefulness to the spring garden – in large groups it resembles a pirouetting dance troupe – but at odds with this poise is the gaudy colour (an incongruity I find thrilling). This orange is probably as bright as a tulip could get, although a closer look reveals an element of nuance. Down the middle of each recurved petal runs a strip of vibrant peach, which gives way at the edges to a tangerine that is infused with yellow. Overall, the effect is like that of a sunset – warm and intense at heart but slowly dissipating as it filters through the surrounding sky.

Planting note: 'Ballerina' works well in a tulip display of analogous reds and yellows. 'Blushing Beauty', 'Amber Glow', 'Prinses Irene' and 'Charade' look attractive mixed alongside.

In-season complementary colour: *Camassia leichtlinii* subsp. *suksdorfii* 'Blauwe Donau' (violet-blue), *Hyacinthus orientalis* 'Delft Blue' (mid-blue), *Muscari aucheri* 'Blue Magic' (powder blue)

In-season analogous colour: *Erysimum* 'Apricot Delight' (apricot), *Erysimum* 'Constant Cheer' (apricot to pink-purple), *Fritillaria imperialis* 'Rubra' (mid-orange)

Beyond Energy

Energetic reds, yellows and oranges share a tumultuous kinship, an understanding that their place in the garden and in the vase is as the ever-affable showmen. Yet, it would be a mistake to assume that their appeal is only ever one-dimensional. This palette comes with a tremendous freedom to experiment with colour, and often the most successful results come from the biggest surprises.

Mid-Purple

Hot oranges and burning ambers – perhaps those from crocosmias, heleniums and sunflowers (*Helianthus*) – find a complement in mid-purple. Opposites on the colour wheel, the two colours work in unison to present a spectacle that is as mysterious as it is blazing. Purple unlocks a depth to orange – a secret layer of intrigue – that can be beneficial in cooling down a floral composition which is perhaps felt to be a little too fiery. In spring, the introduction of honesty (*Lunaria annua*), which flowers in a soft violet, through a parade of smouldering tulips can be effective in bringing a sense of discernment to the planting, and, similarly, in late summer, peppering a hot scheme with drifts of *Verbena bonariensis* can be all that is needed to pull back the intensity of the display.

Electric blue

Electric blue with yellow creates a unique sense of playfulness. The combination has the appearance of two old friends affectionately ribbing each other, each with an understanding of when not to go too far. There is a timelessness in their coupling that I think is best on show in spring: the potent cobalt of *Hyacinthus orientalis* 'Delft Blue' mixed with the purity of sunshine-yellow daffodils, or the powerful ultramarine of the grape hyacinth, *Muscari aucheri* 'Blue Magic', against the canary yellow of crocus. This double act feels so appropriate at the start of the season; it seems to perfectly echo the sense of optimism that comes with an awakening garden and days that are beginning to lengthen.

White

White is a chameleon with the ability to adapt to whatever colour situation it finds itself in. In a muted scheme, its personality becomes compliant and reticent, but as part of an energetic composition, it suddenly finds a hidden exuberance. White, I often think, looks especially compelling with red; somehow its neutrality has the effect of drawing into sharp focus the inherent passion and rapture of red's character. In the garden, it could be umbellifers like Baltic parsley (*Cenolophium denudatum*) or false bishop's weed (*Ammi majus*) wandering through the clarets of *Monarda* 'Cambridge Scarlet' or *Penstemon* 'Windsor Red'. In the vase, it is perhaps the ivory of *Astrantia major* 'Star of Billion' and *Digitalis purpurea* 'Dalmatian White' mixed through the vermillion of *Geum* 'Mrs J. Bradshaw' and *Lupinus* 'Red Rum'.

Left: The playful combination of yellow and blue – here, mixing daffodils with hyacinths and anemones in early spring. Opposite: Spring mix. White and yellow daffodils and mid-purple snake's head fritillaries (*Fritillaria meleagris*) are mixed with the yellows of early spring (primroses, cowslips, daffodils) to create an energetic display with a complex colour profile.

Illustrative Energetic Planting Plan

This energetic planting plan is anchored by dahlias. To the left, 'Bishop of York' begins a sequence that travels across the border through 'Arabian Night', 'Bishop of Auckland' and 'Kelvin Floodlight'. Flowering in a vibrant yellow, a brooding red and a buttery apricot, they set the scene for an understudy of gregarious planting.

The scale brought by the dahlias meets some competition, to the left-hand side, by a moment of bronze *Calamagrostis × acutiflora* 'Karl Foerster'. Yet, while this ornamental grass brings some additional height interest, its main function is to provide textural contrast: where the dahlias are bushy and branching, 'Karl Foerster' is upright and floaty.

The fiery and dramatic orange of *Crocosmia × crocosmiiflora* 'Emily McKenzie' and the sunset colours of *Rudbeckia hirta* 'Autumn Colours' are bounced through the front of the composition to create a blazing tapestry of arching and upright flower interest. From here, on the right-hand side, the ambers and merlots of *Iris* 'Grand Chief' appear through a wave of buttery *Cosmos bipinnatus* 'Xanthos'. This cosmos is one of the lightest values in the composition, which creates a sense of depth by bringing its floaty habit to the foreground.

To the left, *Monarda* 'Cambridge Scarlet' emerges in a drift towards clouds of ivory Baltic parsley (*Cenolophium denudatum*), their diverse textures creating a pleasing play between the statuesque and the billowy. *Cenolophium denudatum* affords the eye a moment of calm, its white flowers allowing a breather amid the riot of colour.

The Mexican sunflower *Tithonia rotundifolia* 'Torch' appears at the back of the border, where its bushy habit complements the dahlias. Its rich orange flowers ricochet between the darker red of *Dahlia* 'Arabian Night' and the unexpected mid-purple of *Verbena bonariensis*. This injection of purple gives the eye a point from which it can explore the surrounding energetic colours. Similar to *Cenolophium denudatum*, *Verbena bonariensis* becomes a kind of landing zone, a palette cleanser to which the eye can return.

Altogether, the scene fizzes with energy – the effects of colour, texture, scale, depth and movement coalescing to evoke an atmosphere of pure vitality.

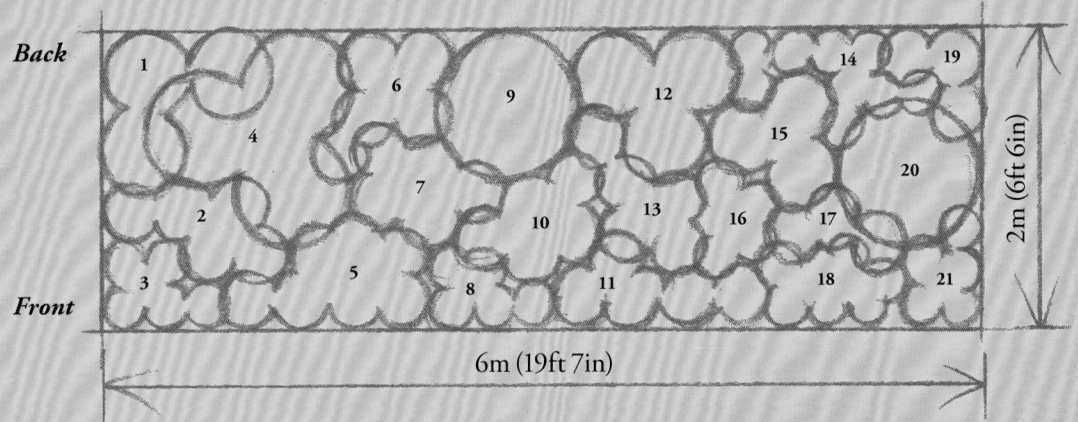

Scale: 1:50
Back / Front
6m (19ft 7in) × 2m (6ft 6in)

1. *Dahlia* 'Bishop of York' × 3
2. *Rudbeckia hirta* 'Autumn Colours' × 5
3. *Crocosmia × crocosmiiflora* 'Emily McKenzie' × 5
4. *Calamagrostis × acutiflora* 'Karl Foerster' × 3
5. *Monarda* 'Cambridge Scarlet' × 7
6. *Tithonia rotundifolia* 'Torch' × 5
7. *Cenolophium denudatum* × 5
8. *Crocosmia × crocosmiiflora* 'Emily McKenzie' × 5
9. *Dahlia* 'Arabian Night' × 1
10. *Geum* 'Totally Tangerine' × 5
11. *Rudbeckia hirta* 'Autumn Colours' × 5
12. *Dahlia* 'Bishop of Auckland' × 3
13. *Cenolophium denudatum* × 5
14. *Verbena bonariensis* × 9
15. *Dahlia* 'Kelvin Floodlight' × 3
16. *Iris germanica* 'Grand Chief' × 5
17. *Cenolophium denudatum* × 3
18. *Cosmos bipinnatus* 'Xanthos' × 7
19. *Tithonia rotundifolia* 'Torch' × 3
20. *Dahlia* 'Arabian Night' × 1
21. *Crocosmia × crocosmiiflora* 'Emily McKenzie' × 5

Notes
This illustrative planting plan would reach its peak in mid-summer and perform best in full sun. Its season of interest could be extended into spring by scattering through tulips such as 'Ballerina', 'Couleur Cardinal' and 'Helmar' or daffodils like *Narcissus* 'Chromacolor' and 'Eaton Song', for example.

Notes on
Energetic Cut Flower Displays

Energetic flower displays make an impact indoors. Where other flowers might be arranged, so they blend seamlessly into the interior or add a polite hint of the outdoors to a dining table, energetic displays look to command attention. They make no apology for their brashness. Instead, they hope to inspire a similar feeling of vigour and vitality in those they come into contact with.

Movement is a key ingredient in energetic arrangements; it is the visual excitement of flowers that interact with one another in compelling and unexpected ways. Perhaps it is rows of daffodils stood to attention in a bowl, or maybe it is arching stems of Solomon's seal (*Polygonatum* × *hybridum*) creating an arresting S-curve. It could be that the impact comes from groups of flowers displayed singularly: a line of bottles each holding a single dahlia stem or a generous collection of bud vases displaying violas. The aim is to surprise, to present flowers in a way that jolts the observer out of the everyday.

In order to achieve these compelling shapes, it is often necessary to think about the mechanics of how everything is held in place. Flower frogs are always my go-to method. Sat at the bottom of a vessel, they allow flowers to be positioned precisely and held with a relative degree of confidence. It is the freedom they offer that makes them so useful: flowers with rigid stems – like lilies, fritillaries and bearded irises (*Iris germanica*) – can be engineered to stand at ninety-degree angles; drooping blooms – like tulips, hyacinths and nasturtiums – can be held, so they cascade elegantly from the sides of their container;

dramatically large foliage can be secured, so it appears to float high above its surroundings. In this respect, flower frogs are perhaps the single most valuable tool I own. However, there are situations where it may be appropriate to use something more rudimentary, like a scrunched-up ball of chicken wire. Taped to the sides of the vessel, chicken wire offers a more robust level of support for heavier stems and flowers that are particularly top-heavy. The key is to first consider the material you are using before any work on the display begins. Are the stems sturdy or do they collapse? Are the flowers balanced on their stem when stood upright or are they too heavy? Next comes the question of shape. What kind of overall composition is desired? What movement will the stems bring to the overall appearance? Answering these questions will inform the choice of support and ensure the display remains stable throughout its creation.

Scale is often a key component of energetic indoor flowers. Large displays are instantly impressive and fill a room with immediate liveliness. But the impact of something more diminutive should not be overlooked. A little pot of marigolds (*Calendula*), fizzing in a blaze of orange, can have as much influence in a room as an oversized jug of sunflowers (*Helianthus*) if positioned in such a way that promotes attention. It might be that the marigolds are displayed on top of a stack of books to lift them off a table, or they may find themselves in a loud vessel that draws the eye towards them. It is about finding those gentle nudges that elevate the flowers to prominence and, in turn, allow the vibrancy of their colour to shine. A little cup of fiery sweet peas (*Lathyrus odoratus*), a jar with a handful of nasturtiums (*Tropaeolum majus*), a bud vase with a single bright orange dahlia: although small in stature, they all share a certain effervescence that is always fun to play with indoors. Ultimately, it is as much about the spirit that flowers emit as it is their physical presence.

Opposite left: A vibrant display of *Narcissus* 'Pipit'. Opposite right: A parade of sunflowers (*Helianthus*) *chez* Marie Varenne, owner of Fleurs d'Arles, in Provence. Above: An energetic mix of cut tulips by a window, including the buttery yellow and blood-red 'Grand Perfection', the white and burgundy 'Rems Favourite', the coppery 'Bronze Perfection', and the creamy, candy floss-pink 'Blushing Lady'.

Above: Drifting clouds of cow parsley (*Anthriscus sylvestris*) by the hedgerows that surround my garden. These frothing, ivory umbellifers create a soft blanket of calm across the whole landscape in early summer. Opposite: A sprawling display of *Aster × frikartii* 'Mönch' in my kitchen. A powdery, pastel blue, its colour is quite unlike anything else in the garden at the start of autumn.

Atmosphere 3:
Reflective

Rain after a spring drought. Tree canopies, newly in leaf, fizz in electric emerald and hedgerows billow into country lanes with vital viridescence. Renewed and hopeful, the sky clears into a wash of brilliant blue, and an eternal serenity descends upon everything across the landscape.

To me, the garden's circus of green is unparalleled in its ability to calm. I feel cocooned and supported among its matrix of verdant foliage, almost as if the colour washes through me and flushes out the unhelpful and distracting noise of everyday life. There is a moment in my garden at some point in late spring, when daffodils and tulips have largely finished and summer interest has not quite got going, where the main colour interest comes solely from masses of leafy green growth. Far from feeling like a lull to me, I have grown to love this brief period of monochromatic tranquillity; somehow it seems necessary and protective, like a long, deep breath before a big performance. I spend a lot of time looking forward when it comes to flowers, anticipating the next curiosity, but this green intermission is really a time when I find myself settling into the reality of the present and discovering joy in the uncomplicated.

Opposite: Reflective scrapbook. The restorative power of green, blue and white – colour that feels essential and instinctive.

Cultivating Calm

Reflection: something that I find in the greens, blues and whites of flowers. But these colours are only one element of the garden and the vase's ability to soothe us. It is often in their synthesis with other, sometimes less tangible, details that a sanctuary of peace and calm is unlocked.

Generations of gardeners have observed the beneficial impact that working with plants and flowers can have on mental well-being, and, for me, it certainly has a profound effect on my ability to rationalize the anxious, confused and unhelpful thoughts that arise from everyday life. The garden becomes a place of safety, a space that belongs only to me, and within it there is a total and unequivocal honesty that I do not find anywhere else. Plants and flowers, for all their majesty, are uncomplicated things; year after year they rise and fall in a predictable rhythm, and they do so free from any judgement or hidden agenda.

Gardens that provide the most soothing moments of reflection always seem to share a common characteristic: a sense of space. This is not always simply in terms of sheer acreage; it can also be in the more abstract way that a small garden appears to offer refuge from a busy outside world. This is a place free from the scrutiny of others, a realm where thoughts can be organized and considered without the influence of endless breaking news, deadlines and modern technology. In these spaces of mental freedom, we are left only to admire the miracle of a fritillary's fascinating chequerboard pattern, a dahlia's exquisite geometry or a rose's romantic ruffle.

The impact of wildlife adds tremendously to an atmosphere of serenity. Encouraging birds, insects and small mammals into the garden reminds us that these are places we look after for the benefit of something bigger, and more fragile, than ourselves. Being a gardener comes with responsibility; we become custodians of a strip of land that we silently agree to preserve for the betterment of nature. On a summer's afternoon, there is no greater joy than the circus of wildlife that a thoughtfully planted garden brings. There are blackbirds hunting spiders, butterflies floating between flowers, bees busying themselves collecting nectar, and grasshoppers leaping from foliage hideouts; dragonflies, slowworms, caterpillars, beetles and all manner of other weird-and-wonderful critters are also liable to join the fray. Simply observing – even for just a few moments each day – the little dramas created by these tiny organisms has an overwhelmingly calming effect, at least on me.

Opposite: The calming cobalt of *Hyacinthus orientalis* 'Delft Blue' displayed against a wall in complementary orange.

There is a recognition that no matter how complicated and chaotic our daily lives may seem, we really belong to a simpler and more innocent world.

The reflective gardener takes comfort from the clarity of flower colour. Where other aspects of life may be uncertain, all the tints, tones and shades that emerge throughout the year have an unquestionable purity. When, after a long winter, the first primroses start to pepper sleeping hedgerows, it is hard not to feel reassured by the sincerity with which their butter-yellow petals brighten the landscape, and when, in mid- to late spring, old pheasant's eye daffodils (*Narcissus poeticus* var. *recurvus*) appear among a riot of tulips, it is impossible not to find an honesty within their glossy, white flowers. The garden's hues are presented to us without ulterior motive; their only ambition is that they might be given the chance to do it all again next year.

∗

There is nothing quite like the sense of mental clarity that spending time in someone else's garden brings to me. There is a freedom to do nothing, to enjoy the experience of being cocooned by flowers and foliage without the persistent agitation I feel in my own garden to be doing something to make improvements. When I'm in my own space there are always plants that could be cut back or staked, deadheading to get on top of, a greenhouse to be cleaned, and paths to be swept; for all the undoubtedly great benefits it brings to my life and my mental well-being, I am not sure I can ever truly relax in the company of my own planting.

This is why visiting homes and gardens that I find particularly calming, like those that follow, is so important to me. With a detachment from ownership comes the ability to surrender to the magic of flowers.

Above right: The timeless purity of *Narcissus papyraceus* displayed in my library.
Right: Textural greens surround steps at Perrycroft in the Malvern Hills. Opposite: A display of foxgloves (*Digitalis purpurea*) in pinks and creamy whites in early summer.

Above: Garden party flowers in front of a playful ODD Limited rocker. *Ammi majus* and *Bupleurum rotundifolium* create a floaty display of ivory and chartreuse.
Opposite: A dreamy mix of *Alchemilla mollis*, *Centaurea cyanus*, St John's wort (*Hypericum perforatum*) and delphiniums at Tilley Printing in Ledbury.

A Slice of Country in London
Butter Wakefield

COLOUR PROFILE:
*Vital greens, billowing ivory and powdered blue.
A haven of delicate violets and grounded sage.*

Taking the District Line to west London is about as urban an experience as you could ever likely get. The screeching of metal on metal, the warm smell of grease, a never-ending wave of people busied with deadlines and appointments; it is the city at its most brilliantly messy. You would be forgiven for thinking that the bucolic serenity of the country was far out of reach here, but there is a place, not far from where the River Thames makes a sharp U-bend through Chiswick and Hammersmith, that offers a soothing sanctuary.

It is the home of garden designer Butter Wakefield, a place so generously layered and softened by flowers that the echoes of surrounding concrete chaos are instantly replaced by gentle and calming whispers of tranquillity. The house is a melting pot of textures. Upholstery, paintings, antiques, keepsakes and fabrics all coalesce to create charming and highly personal rooms. There is a real sense of leaving the regular world behind in favour of a journey through Butter's eclectic and whimsical imagination.

The garden is accessed from the kitchen, a room filled with ceramics, works of art and all manner of curiosities. It is a lesson in maximizing space, in not letting the confines of an urban plot dampen creativity.

Opposite: Running down the lawn of Butter's garden is an endlessly soothing wildflower meadow that in late spring is punctuated here and there with alliums.

Above: Statement shrubs in containers flank the back door, and each is underplanted with a lush carpet of verdant texture. Here, Mexican fleabane (*Erigeron karvinskianus*) creates a frothing understorey to the interest above.
Opposite: A delightful display of foxgloves (*Digitalis purpurea*) in Butter's sitting room.

Statement shrubs like *Osmanthus × burkwoodii* are generously underplanted with ferns and other shade-loving perennials in large terracotta pots on the terrace. These have the effect of framing the view out onto the garden from the back door and allow for interest to be extended outside the main planted borders. These borders trace the edges of the garden and are deep enough to accommodate a wonderfully layered composition of perennials, structural shrubs and playful topiary. They billow beside a central lawn that for the most part has been given over to a thrilling wildflower meadow down its centre.

'My garden is a place that offers me the most profound amount of peace and sense of calm,' Butter tells me. 'It amuses and occupies when I am at my lowest.' All gardens, I would argue, have an inherent ability to calm, but there is something about this one, in the heart of a major capital city, that feels particularly restorative. Some Londoners book expensive spa treatments or travel to far-flung places around the world in search of the peace of mind that the city so easily grinds down, when really all that is needed is half an hour spent here.

Flowers from the garden routinely find their way inside. Their display on tables and worktops reinforces a sense of the home's isolation from the melee of surrounding London – this is a place that the metropolitan sprawl cannot penetrate. Butter's extensive collection of antique jugs and vases are filled with whatever is flowering outside to create little garden vignettes. It is a Sunday evening activity, a time to relax after the chores of the weekend have been completed:

'I feel the most relaxed on Sunday evening when I have had both days to do my weekly chores: the tidy up, mow the lawn, pick up the endless *Magnolia grandiflora* leaves and collect a few flowers for a small jug or two to help ease me back into the coming week ahead. The satisfaction – it's almost relief – I feel is thorough and very happy-making!'

Each time I visit this urban refuge, it is the soothing influence of green that I take away with me. It permeates from the rich tapestry of foliage in the garden and seems to drape like a comforting blanket across the rooms inside, an abstract sense of becoming wrapped in a viridescent embrace. Total serenity.

Opposite, clockwise from top left: *Aquilegia* 'Rose Queen' brings a cottagey feel to Butter's urban garden; *Tulipa* 'Marilyn', with wonderful ivory petals flushed with scarlet; layers of texture in Butter's garden; a display of *Tulipa* 'Fire Wings' lights up the sitting room. Overleaf: *Allium hollandicum* 'Purple Sensation' drifting through the wildflower meadow.

A Voysey Fairy Tale
Gillian Archer

COLOUR PROFILE:
*Zestful green and pearlescent white.
An arcadia of earthy and essential limes, shamrocks and olives.*

In the hills just north of Ledbury, in Herefordshire, an extraordinary Arts and Crafts country home has overlooked the Iron Age hill fort of British Camp for the last 130 years. Designed by Charles F A Voysey in the late 19th century, Perrycroft was one of the celebrated architect's first major commissions and bears early examples of a style that would go on to define his legacy.

Today, the house is the home of Gillian Archer and her husband Mark. It sits in some 80 acres on the western slopes of the Malvern Hills, and in typical Arts and Crafts style, there is a certain harmony between the property, the garden and the landscape. Characteristic of Voysey's domestic architecture, Perrycroft is a house that in its functional simplicity and low horizontal lines is careful not to impose itself too harshly on the surrounding environment. Whitewashed roughcast walls, a sweeping slate roof and large bay windows are, again, typical of the architect and gloriously preserved here. All trims – window frames, doors, downpipes – are painted in an earthy sap green that adds a playful decorative edge to the largely utilitarian style of the property.

Opposite: *Rosa* Jayne Austin ('Ausbreak') is mixed informally through lady's mantle (*Alchemilla mollis*), phlox and feverfew (*Tanacetum parthenium*).

Opposite: Lush, textural planting is contained by low clipped hedging and punctuated by topiary to create a juxtaposition of formal and informal elements. Above: In a mixed bed, the bright yellow of *Kniphofia* 'Sunningdale Yellow' pierces a reflective palette of powdery blue phlox and ivory *Verbascum chaixii* 'Album'.

The garden is a wonderful mix of formal and informal elements, which is completely in tune with the Arts and Crafts ethos of the house. As Gillian explained to me:

'I have always enjoyed the cottage garden style, with its natural plant associations, but on the other hand, I love the discipline of formal gardens – hedges and topiary can be incredibly satisfying. The two come together perfectly with the Arts and Crafts ideal… which is so appropriate for our garden…a formal structure and very loose planting.'

'Rooms' cascade down a steep slope from the front of the house, journeying through parterres, cottage beds, long borders, meadows and an orchard. Closest to the house there is an informal courtyard space, which in summer froths with dramatic waves of self-seeded lady's mantle (*Alchemilla mollis*). Box (*Buxus sempervirens*) clipped into triangles and oblongs is dotted throughout and provides an interesting contrast to the incredibly loose composition of perennials that surround them. From here, a large yew (*Taxus baccata*) hedge (with finials clipped into bird shapes) leads to an area containing parterres, which are flanked by impressive topiary sculptures. Generously planted long borders surround the space, and, by virtue of its elevated position, a view of boundless, undulating country is borrowed as a glorious backdrop.

Inspiration has come from various places, which speaks to the garden's exciting mix of ideas. Gillian cites other Arts and Crafts schemes as influential – such as Lytes Cary Manor, in Somerset, and Hidcote, in Gloucestershire – but trips to Italy visiting Villa Cetinale, in Tuscany, and Ninfa near Rome (both historic Italian gardens with English influences in the planting) have also shaped her work at Perrycroft. Reading is also important, and when I speak with Gillian, she quickly reels off a list of key works:

'Christopher Lloyd, especially *The Well-Tempered Garden*; Russell Page's *The Education of a Gardener*; the writings of Graham Stuart Thomas, Vita Sackville-West and Rosemary Verey. Also, Mirabel Osler's *A Gentle Plea for Chaos*.'

This is a place of quiet innovation. A house and garden preserved and cultivated with incredible passion that never, in the spirit of its original philosophy, seek the limelight too vehemently. There is an incredible sense of peace here, a serenity that seems to radiate from the house, down through the garden and linger among the neighbouring hills.

Far left: A dramatic display of *Ammi majus*, *Alchemilla mollis* and bells of Ireland (*Moluccella laevis*) in the stables. Left: The common spotted orchid (*Dactylorhiza fuchsii*) popping up through grass in a wilder area of the garden. Opposite: Perrycroft scrapbook.

The Magic of Restraint
Kettle's Yard

COLOUR PROFILE:
*Honest ivory, earthy green and grounded ochre.
A sanctuary of quiet pastels.*

Sometimes the most evocative of places eschew the fussiness of colour and pattern. They carve a lighter path, creating neutral spaces that encourage the imagination to fill in the blanks. Kettle's Yard, the former home of Jim Ede (a curator at the Tate in London in the early 20th century) and his wife Helen, is one such place, and its simplicity is a sobering lesson in restraint.

Jim and Helen moved to Cambridge in the mid-1950s and set about converting four small and dilapidated 19th-century cottages on the immediate outskirts of the city centre into one home. This was to be more than just a place to live; it was also to serve as a gallery for Jim's extensive art collection, amassed through the connections and friendships he had made while working at the Tate. The Edes had a very clear aesthetic vision, which hinged on the principles of simplicity, harmony and balance, and it was this philosophy that shaped the pared-back and unpretentious interiors at Kettle's Yard.

The rooms at Kettle's Yard are whitewashed and furniture is sparse. Where there are tables, chairs and cabinets, they are functional and unembellished. This is a place where the frivolous frills of decoration are rejected in favour of the calming tranquillity that comes with prudence.

Opposite: A simple display of lady's mantle (*Alchemilla mollis*) on the dining table at Kettle's Yard. The sparsity of the interior, in terms of both its furnishings and colour, creates a calming and neutral stage for cut flowers.

Writing in his 1984 book *A Way of Life*, Jim described his approach to the interiors at Kettle's Yard as something of a meditation:

'I like to keep very quiet in a room, and to have it always still; for this reason I want it to be orderly. It is to me as if it were a pool of silence, and just as a pool when stirred loses its transparency, so a room is stirred by movement. Most people's rooms are like hurricanes.'

Where there is colour, it comes in the form of art. Work by Joan Miró leaps in watery cobalt from the ivory walls of the sitting room. A murky still life of cut flowers by Christopher Wood has the same effect by one of the windows. It is this punctuation of paintings and sculptures across the living spaces that stops the home from feeling clinical and overly sanitized. Instead, the sense is of an environment thoughtfully considered to provide an unsullied backdrop to the impressive art collection.

Flowers in this environment go one of two ways: they either blend into the neutrality of the interior and become lost or they use the lucidity of their surroundings as a springboard from which to pop. It is easy to imagine how a small cup of snowdrops (*Galanthus*) in winter or a little vase of primroses in spring could lose their impact; of course, they would still bring a pretty sense of softness to the room, but their performance would not be terribly forthcoming. In contrast, larger, more keenly saturated flowers – perhaps tulips, dahlias, zinnias – use this kind of space to their advantage. Free from distraction, their colours, shapes and textures take on a heightened sense of drama.

There is a small, charming garden at Kettle's Yard that wraps around the house. It consists of a simple stone path travelling through small pockets of mixed planting. When first created by the Edes in the mid-20th century, they planted Mediterranean shrubs like lavender and rosemary (perhaps inspired by their years living in Tangier, Morocco), alongside fruit trees (there are two medlars) and a series of climbing roses. Today, the garden is maintained by the Kettle's Yard Trust, who every week in spring and summer use it to collect cut flowers for display across the house. These displays are largely kept simple and unelaborate; in keeping, I suppose, with the house's overall atmosphere of sobriety.

Previous pages, clockwise from top left: Artfully displayed pebbles collected by Jim Ede; a collection of houseplants and glassware displayed by an upstairs window; displays of Icelandic poppy (*Oreomecon nudicaulis*) melt into the sober interior; the charming 12th-century St Peter's church overlooking the garden; the sweeping first floor landing decorated simply with blue-and-white platters. Opposite: A dramatic display of delphiniums in electric blue echoes the hanging antique witch's ball in the window.

Opposite: The restrained interior is a perfect companion to the timeless simplicity of lady's mantle (*Alchemilla mollis*). Above: A blousy moment of powder-pink peonies adds a sense of romance to the muted interior.

Serenity in Provence
Atelier Vime

COLOUR PROFILE:
Earthy ochre, grounded terracotta and warm ivory.
A warren of dusty blues, muddied yellows and olive-greens.

In southern France, the charming village of Vallabrègues sits beside the mighty Rhône as it makes its final advance to the Mediterranean. Largely unknown to tourists, this sleepy place is authentic and unspoilt Provence: villagers enjoy games of *pétanque* in sandy areas under the shade of beech trees and a charming café serves pastis to locals.

Vallabrègues has a long history of basket weaving – in the 19th century it was the largest basket-producing area in France – and although nowadays the industry has declined, its legacy is kept alive through a summer festival, a museum and, most notably, the Atelier Vime workshop.

Founded by Anthony Watson and Benoît Rauzy, Atelier Vime centres around an early-18th-century *hôtel particulier*, which overlooks the point at which the Rhône and the Gardon converge. A former wicker workshop, the house is a time capsule from a period of immense prosperity in the basketry trade, and now serves as the pair's showroom, shop and home. Although this place is layered with antique furniture, fabrics, books and ceramics, it retains a sense of space and airiness, offering a light and capacious retreat from the most intense of the Provençal heat.

Opposite: In the cool, calming air of the sitting room, cosmos are displayed in a rattan Atelier Vime Médici vase. Overleaf, from left to right: An ethereal display of *Ammi majus* sits in front of an antique tapestry depicting Alexander the Great entering Babylon; a handful of sunflowers (*Helianthus*) picked from the garden and displayed in an antique blue-and-white urn in one of the bedrooms.

Below: A single stem of *Cosmos bipinnatus* 'Candy Stripe' displayed on a mantlepiece. Opposite, clockwise from top left: Clouds of ivory cosmos in the courtyard; more sunflowers displayed in a bathroom; a charming wall sconce vase with dried flowers; bougainvillea surrounding the pool.

A cobbled courtyard sits to the front of the house and is a place of simple charm. Old benches are adorned with potted plants, ceramic bowls and glass cloches, while a simple bistro table and chairs creates a delightful summer breakfast spot before the sun becomes too overpowering. To the side, and curiously hidden behind an old stone wall, there is an enchanting small pool, which is canopied by a climbing bougainvillea with masses of flowers in a delicious candy pink. Consumed by the sound of cicadas and drenched in the warmth of a Mediterranean summer, these outdoor spaces are not only wonderfully evocative but also highly tranquil. As Anthony himself describes, they provide precious moments of calm and promote clarity of thought throughout the day:

'The coolness of morning on the terrace…afternoons by the pool… dusk as the sun brushes the cobblestones…Even though we work here, these spaces still retain a special atmosphere that inspires us.'

Inside, the rooms are large with high ceilings and generous windows. They are filled with paintings, sculptures and all manner of *objets d'art*: heirloom tapestries hang above party invitations from Jean Cocteau; traditional Provençal dishes are displayed alongside Delft tiles and antique busts; art and books spill from cabinets, tables and mantlepieces. Everything is held together casually. There is no preoccupation with neatness. Instead, there is a certain sincerity in the acceptance of imperfection. The disorder never appears frenzied or chaotic; in fact, despite the generous assemblage of textures and shapes, rooms have a distinct sense of serenity.

Cut flowers have a dreamy and ethereal feel in this space, floating through rooms with a celestial elegance. They find homes against the crumbly, breathy blues of ageing walls and the buttered ivories of 18th-century stone masonry. In many ways they feel less like transitory guests from the garden and more like permanent, vital components of the overall decoration. The palette here is warm and comforting; colours across the house are tempered by the most golden and unblemished of southern light.

Reflective Flower Colour
Blue, Green, White

Nothing compares to the comfort of blue and green. No other two colours are as essential; no other two colours are as rudimentary. In our primitive minds they symbolize everything that we recognize as good and safe about life on this planet. If we were to rocket ourselves many hundreds of thousands of miles into the black abyss of space and then turn around, we would look back at our Earth and notice that our infinitely colourful world is suddenly reduced to its two most primal factors; we would see a planet, beautiful and fragile, shining in blue and green.

These colours are the garden at its most fundamental, the foundations on which all other building blocks rest. Without green how could we ever contemplate a red or an orange? Without blue how could we ever possibly dream of a yellow? If there was no white, how could there ever be any colour at all? I suppose it is this sense of indispensability – these colours as an elixir of life – that connects with a basic and elemental instinct inside me; there is a comfort and reassurance in their necessity.

In many ways, blue and green are easily overlooked in planting and indoor cut flower displays: green because of its ubiquity and blue because of its relative scarcity. However, for their ability, along with white, to bring an effortless sense of serenity to both the garden and the house they deserve far greater consideration.

Opposite: Reflective blues and greens offer me an incomparable feeling of comfort. Here, the pastel blues of the sweetpeas, *Lathyrus odoratus* 'Bristol' and 'Noel Sutton' combine with the chartreuse of lady's mantle (*Alchemilla mollis*) and the cobalt of cornflowers (*Centaurea cyanus*).

Blue

Everyone likes blue. Men, women, young, old, European, American; no matter our differences, studies from across the world show that we all appear to unite in a fondness for this primary colour, repeatedly citing it as our favourite. If our preferences are explained by Ecological Valence Theory – the principle that favoured hues remind us of pleasant objects, places, people and situations from our past – it is easy to see why blue should enjoy such universal adoration on account of the fact that it is almost impossible to think of anything negative, in the naturally occurring world at least, that can be associated with it. Instead, our primitive minds are taken to images that have for millennia stirred a basic survival instinct and instilled a deep-rooted sense of safety: clear skies and fresh water. No matter how sophisticated we believe ourselves to be, we are still driven by the same impulses that have ensured our survival and prosperity on this planet for hundreds of thousands of years.

When compared to the pervasiveness of other colours, blue in the garden – or at least a blue that could not also be considered a kind of purple – is relatively rare. Flicking through a seed catalogue or nursery brochure, blues will always be in short supply, especially for interest in late summer and early autumn. To me, blue is a flower colour most associated with the rush of new life in spring. Suddenly there is the breathy cyan of grape hyacinths (*Muscari*), *Iris reticulata* and *Scilla siberica* alongside the more intense cobalt of English bluebells (*Hyacinthoides non-scripta*) and hyacinths. Seemingly from nowhere, and only for this fleeting moment, this once scarce hue dances in abundance through planting and finds its way into all manner of displays inside the house.

Opposite: Blue scrapbook. A year of tranquillity.

Plant Profiles: Restorative Blue

*Life's elixir. The comfort of a sparkling summer sky.
Colour at its most soothing.*

Centaurea cyanus (cornflower)

Annual • Summer • Height: 90cm (35in), spread: up to 50cm (20in) • Full sun • All soil types except very heavy clay • Vase life: excellent (1+ week) • Flower colour value: mid-to-dark

Cornflowers are gloriously old-fashioned, the sort of flowers that infuse my head with dreams of hidden cottage gardens filled with colour. Nowadays they are easily overshadowed by glamorous perennials and more sophisticated annuals, which is a shame as not only do they bring great texture to the garden and the vase, but their colour is also so pure and soothing. It is a blue that journeys from light to dark. At the flower's throat, stamens are arranged in a puffball of deep indigo; here the blue leans towards purple and has a depth that draws the eye into its centre. The surrounding petals feel different; they have an icy quality, a blue that is cool and diluted. Together, they create a complex flower that is ever-changing depending on the light.

Planting note: Cornflowers look attractive in drifts through summer perennials – their loose habit plays well against more upright and structural plants like lupins, salvias and phlomis.

In-season complementary colour: *Calendula officinalis* 'Indian Prince' (mid-orange), *Eschscholzia californica* 'Orange King' (mid-orange), *Tropaeolum majus* Jewel of Africa Group (mid-orange)

In-season analogous colour: *Agapanthus campanulatus* 'Cobalt Blue' (mid-blue), *Phacelia campanularia* (mid-blue), *Rosa* Munstead Wood ('Ausbernard') (merlot)

Geranium Rozanne (hardy geranium)

Perennial • Summer • Height: up to 1m (39in), spread: up to 1m (39in) • Full sun to partial shade • All soil types • Vase life: excellent (1+ week) • Flower colour value: light-to-mid

Hardy geraniums are incredibly valuable plants in the summer garden. Loose, informal and flowering profusely, they add a soft and relaxed texture to a planting scheme and look particularly effective as underplanting for larger shrubs and trees. *Geranium* Rozanne is an outstanding cultivar that bears masses of cup-shaped blooms for a long period into autumn. Its petals are a dusty blue at the edges but fade to a creamy lilac at the centre. In large groups the flowers create thrilling undulating waves of cobalt that look quite unlike anything else in the garden at any other time.

Planting note: All hardy geraniums look attractive as understudies to larger statement plants. I particularly enjoy seeing powdery pink shrub roses like Emily Brontë ('Ausearnshaw') and Scepter'd Isle ('Ausland') underplanted with *Geranium* Rozanne.

In-season complementary colour: *Geum* 'Totally Tangerine' (tangerine), *Iris germanica* 'William of Orange' (peach), *Rosa* Lady of Shalott ('Ausnyson') (apricot)

In-season analogous colour: *Allium hollandicum* 'Purple Sensation' (mid-purple), *Nigella damascena* 'Miss Jekyll' (sky-blue), *Phacelia campanularia* (mid-blue)

Iris × *robusta* 'Gerald Darby'

Perennial • Summer • Height: up to 90cm (35in), spread: up to 50cm (20in) • Full sun to partial shade • Thrives in permanently moist soil or shallow water • Vase life: good (up to 1 week) • Flower colour value: mid

'Gerald Darby' is a marginal pond plant, thriving in boggy soils or shallow water. All irises, I think, have an inherent elegance, but this cultivar seems to take gracefulness to a new level. Rising on slender stems above a mound of sword-like foliage, its petals are wonderfully crinkled and give the flower a charming sense of informality. Standards are a light, powdery blue that leans towards violet and fades to a kind of magenta at the base, while the falls are pure cobalt with a flash of complementary canary-yellow through the centre. Overall, this flower has a finesse that feels terribly sophisticated.

Planting note: Planted at pond margins, 'Gerald Darby' provides a delightful transition between the water feature and the wider ornamental garden. I always think they look best in groups of at least five to allow their soothing colour to rhythmically drift along the water's edge.

In-season complementary colour: *Kniphofia* 'Incandesce' (mid-orange), *Tithonia rotundifolia* 'Torch' (mid-orange), *Zinnia elegans* 'Orange King' (mid-orange)

In-season analogous colour: *Allium hollandicum* 'Purple Sensation' (mid-purple), *Digitalis purpurea* (mid-pink), *Nepeta racemosa* 'Walker's Low' (violet-blue)

Nigella damascena 'Miss Jekyll' (love-in-a-mist)

Annual • Summer • Height: up to 50cm (20in), spread: up to 10cm (4in) • Full sun to partial shade • All soil types • Vase life: excellent (1+ week) • Flower colour value: light-to-mid

In a cottage garden scheme there are, for me, a handful of annuals that are non-negotiable. Sweet peas would definitely be one, but so too would nigella. There is nothing quite like the floaty and ethereal blanket of calm they provide when allowed to meander informally through the early summer garden. 'Miss Jekyll' is a cultivar that flowers in a dreamy sky-blue. Like a sapphire cushion, its simple petals are arranged in layers around extended stamens, with the colour becoming more saturated at the lower level. The flowers are, of course, a highlight, but the bulb-like seedheads (an apple-green flushed with purple) also extends their interest through the season.

Planting note: 'Miss Jekyll' will freely self-seed in favourable conditions. Personally, I find the informal clusters that this creates thrilling, but in a garden where there is a desire to keep tight control over the planting, some maintenance will be required to contain its performance.

In-season complementary colour: *Calendula officinalis* 'Indian Prince' (mid-orange), *Geum* 'Totally Tangerine' (tangerine), *Lathyrus odoratus* 'Prince of Orange' (coral)

In-season analogous colour: *Lathyrus odoratus* 'Blue Velvet' (deep purple), *Salvia nemorosa* 'Caradonna' (violet-purple), *Scabiosa* 'Butterfly Blue' (mauve)

Green

Green, a secondary colour, takes the authority of blue and combines it with the playfulness of yellow. Yet, despite its blended provenance, it feels distinctly independent. The other primary fusions seem to make instinctive sense – orange feels a natural result of red and yellow; purple seems completely in tune with red and blue – but with green there is a mystery. Green has a certain self-sufficiency that suggests it should be a primary itself, as though nothing else could possibly have created such an autonomous hue.

In the garden, green is non-specific; there is no way of ever truly summarizing its overall characteristic because the multitude of tints, tones and shades is so endless. It can be dark and subdued like the foliage of yew (*Taxus baccata*) or acidic and sparkling like the chartreuse of euphorbia. There are occasions when it is glaucous – as in the case of some hostas and the opium poppy (*Papaver somniferum*) – alongside moments of brilliant, unsullied boldness, such as the gutsy and decisive summer leaves of zinnias and crocosmias. As green so often becomes the neutral backdrop to garden planting and cut flower displays, interest is created when a mix of all these variations is woven through the composition; green in this way becomes a tapestry of texture.

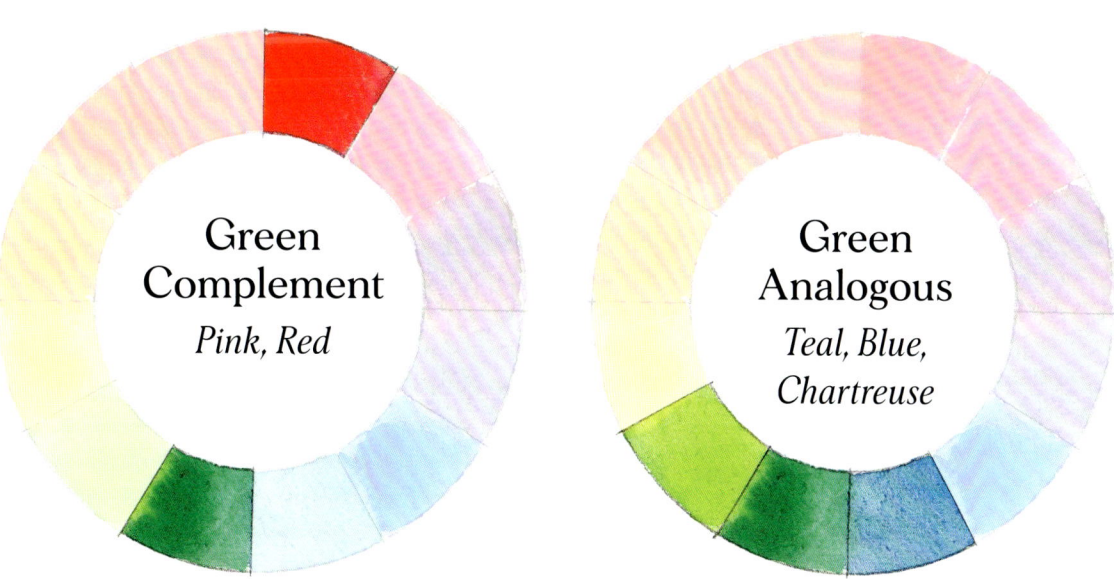

Green scrapbook. Inescapable, essential and endlessly calming; a year in green is far from boring.

Plant Profiles: Essential Green

The miracle of life. Terrestrial. Lush, luxurious and abundant, this is the colour of growth and renewal. The calming and reassuring comfort of home.

Alchemilla mollis (lady's mantle)

Perennial • Summer • Height: up to 60cm (24in), spread: 80cm (32in) • Full sun to full shade • All soil types • Vase life: excellent (1+ week) • Flower colour value: light-to-mid

Some plants are so reliable that I can never imagine a planting scheme in any garden without them. For the simplicity of its flowers and foliage, its bushy and spreading habit, and its ability to thrive in almost any garden, *Alchemilla mollis* would perhaps be at the top of this list. For me, its leaves are as treasured as its blooms. The scalloped discs first appear like small stars before expanding into platters of forest-green, and they are rightly famed for the way water droplets rest on their surface like little pearls. Unfussy flowers emerge on spindly stems in informal sprays to create a rich texture, but it is their colour that I find most extraordinary. It is an acidic chartreuse, a zesty lime that cuts through all other surrounding greens.

Planting note: I love *Alchemilla mollis* for its tendency to self-seed, finding nooks and crannies everywhere in the garden. Its spread can be prolific, so ongoing maintenance is required if this is not desired or space does not allow.

In-season complementary colour: *Rosa* Sir John Betjeman ('Ausvivid') (cerise), *Rosa* Thomas à Becket ('Auswinston') (ruby), *Salvia* 'Royal Bumble' (mid-red)

In-season analogous colour: *Angelica archangelica* (chartreuse), *Nicotiana langsdorffii* (chartreuse), *Phacelia campanularia* (mid-blue)

Angelica archangelica

Biennial • Summer • Height: up to 2m (6ft 6in), spread: 1.2m (4ft) • Partial shade • All soil types except very heavy clay • Vase life: excellent (1+ week) • Flower colour value: light-to-mid

A biennial (or short-lived perennial), *Angelica archangelica* is capable of reaching around 2m (6ft 6in) in height. Towering above the emerging foliage of early summer perennials, the whole plant is a celebration of green. In early spring, large leaves appear in a shade of olive before incredibly robust, scaffold-like stems push skyward in a lighter apple tone. Crowning the plant are umbels of flowers in a punchy chartreuse; it is a citrusy green that borrows significantly from yellow, so that in bright, midday light the ping-pong-ball blooms almost appear to be a kind of lemon-yellow.

Planting note: *Angelica archangelica* is a statement plant that requires space for its full performance to be admired. It looks attractive emerging from a carpet of foliage in contrasting textures – *Luzula nivea* and hardy geraniums are a good choice.

In-season complementary colour: *Geum* 'Mrs J. Bradshaw' (vermillion), *Iris germanica* 'Sultan's Palace' (rust-red), *Penstemon* 'Red Riding Hood' (mid-red)

In-season analogous colour: *Alchemilla mollis* (chartreuse), *Digitalis grandiflora* (lemon-yellow), *Iris germanica* 'Benton Apollo' (lemon-yellow)

Euphorbia amygdaloides var. *robbiae* (wood spurge)

Perennial • Spring to summer • Height: up to 70cm (28in), spread: up to 1m (39in) • Full sun to full shade • All soil types except very heavy clay • Vase life: good (up to 1 week) • Flower colour value: mid

There are many wonderful varieties of euphorbia, from the tall and dramatic *Euphorbia characias* subsp. *wulfenii* to the delightfully diminutive *E. epithymoides*, but one that I hold in high esteem for its adaptability to any garden and the colour of its flowers is *Euphorbia amygdaloides* var. *robbiae*. This mid-size variety can spread quickly in shady areas to produce an interesting textural carpet. Its leaves are dramatically dark, a kind of bottle green, and provide a shadowy understorey above which sprays of flowers froth in a punchy lime.

Planting note: *Euphorbia amygdaloides* var. *robbiae* is a valuable plant for shade and creates much-needed interest under trees and larger shrubs. Mixing shade-tolerant annuals and biennials like *Lunaria annua* and *Digitalis* through their carpet always looks attractive in early summer.

In-season complementary colour: *Anemone coronaria* 'Hollandia' (mid-red), *Tulipa* 'Apeldoorn' (mid-red), *Tulipa* 'Armani' (ruby)

In-season analogous colour: *Euphorbia epithymoides* (chartreuse), *Narcissus* 'Eaton Song' (mid-yellow), *Narcissus* 'Tahiti' (butter-yellow)

Polygonatum × *hybridum* (Solomon's seal)

Perennial • Spring • Height: up to 1.2m (4ft), spread: up to 50cm (20in) • Full sun to full shade • All soil types • Vase life: excellent (1+ week) • Flower colour value: mid

One of my favourite plants for building textural intrigue is *Polygonatum* × *hybridum*. Its arching stems provide a layered and architectural focal point to a shady area of the garden or a collection of cut flowers in the house. Leaves are a solid and unequivocal mid-green, the sort of green that feels vital, and it is largely for this foliage that I admire the plant so highly. Its flowers are pretty – like little ivory pearls dipped in emerald at the tips – but they often become lost under the surrounding verdant canopy.

Planting note: *Polygonatum* × *hybridum* looks attractive mixed with ferns, hostas and *Alchemilla mollis* under trees and larger shrubs. However, it is important that the plant is given adequate space to ensure that its acrobatic, arching performance reaches its full potential.

In-season complementary colour: *Geum* 'Mrs J. Bradshaw' (vermillion), *Iris germanica* 'Sultan's Palace' (rust-red), *Papaver* Red Rumble (mid-red)

In-season analogous colour: *Alchemilla mollis* (chartreuse), *Iris germanica* 'Benton Apollo' (lemon-yellow), *Nicotiana langsdorffii* (chartreuse)

White

White is the ultimate enigma. What is it hiding? Surely there is something hidden beneath the absoluteness of its impartiality, a depth that leans warm or cold, friendly or hostile? Perhaps, as a reflection of all light wavelengths, the answer lies in its status as the culmination of all colours: could white, in fact, be everything all at once? Graceful and aggressive. Sedate and energetic. Happy and sad.

With flowers, white's neutrality has a tremendous ability to root me in the present. When I observe an ivory daffodil (*Narcissus*) or mounds of twinkling snowdrops (*Galanthus*), my mind is uniquely focused on the here and now; all other distractions – the stresses and anxieties of everyday life – seem for those few moments to melt away into a void of insignificance. In this way, pearly white blooms drifting through the garden or rippling like meringue through a cut display are more than just decorative to me; they are, without exaggeration, a therapy.

White scrapbook. Frothy, sparkling and celestial, the white garden often feels like the ultimate luxury.

ATMOSPHERE 3: REFLECTIVE

Plant Profiles: Ethereal White

Dreamy and celestial, the colour of innocence. A blank canvas on which all life's messy ups and downs is written. A fresh start. Colour at its most uncolourful.

Cenolophium denudatum (Baltic parsley)

Perennial • Summer • Height: up to 1m (39in), spread: up to 50cm (20in) • Full sun to partial shade • All soil types • Vase life: good (up to 1 week) • Flower colour value: light

I am a huge fan of umbellifers of all kinds. There is something about the floaty informality of their long stems and saucer-shaped, powdery flowers that captures a romantic instinct in my imagination. I am incredibly fond of the annual *Ammi majus*, but perhaps my all-time favourite is *Cenolophium denudatum*. A robust perennial, it adds textural interest to planted beds and cut displays year after year and is one of the plants that I most look forward to as its feathery foliage begins to emerge in spring. Leaves are dissected and appear in profusion at the base of the plant in a glossy forest-green. From there, flexible, darker stems rise to 90cm (35in) and carry masses of lacy flowers in a chalky white.

Planting note: *Cenolophium denudatum* is an excellent plant for filling gaps with textural interest. Largely fuss-free, the flowers can sometimes become top-heavy and cause the stems to droop, so some light staking is occasionally required.

Iris orientalis (Turkish iris)

Perennial • Summer • Height: up to 1m (39in), spread: up to 50cm (20in) • Full sun to partial shade • All soil types except very heavy clay • Vase life: good (up to 1 week) • Flower colour value: light

Iris orientalis is not as showy as its bearded iris peers but, for me, its simplicity marks a welcome change of pace. Tall, slender and robust, the mid-green stems rise to around 1m (39in) in early summer and support sword-like leaves that give the plant an imposing and dramatic silhouette. Up to five flowers emerge in a cascade down the stem, each with slightly crinkled petals. Both standards and falls are a creamy ivory, but where the standards have the slightest hint of butter running up the centre, the falls carry a saturated and unmistakeable splash of lemon.

Planting note: *Iris orientalis* looks attractive popping up through summer perennials that have contrasting habits to its upright posture. The bushiness of hardy geraniums, the sprawling informality of shrub roses, and the loose informality of *Nepeta* make exciting neighbours.

Narcissus poeticus var. *recurvus* (old pheasant's eye)

Perennial bulb • Late spring • Height: up to 40cm (16in), spread: up to 10cm (4in) • Full sun to partial shade • All soil types • Vase life: excellent (1+ week) • Flower colour value: light

Just when you think the last of the *Narcissus* has been and gone, replaced by the candy-shop riot of tulips, along comes *Narcissus poeticus* var. *recurvus*. Its late flowering seems to take me by surprise every year (my head having shifted to summer perennials), so that when they arrive, I am always thrown back into a narcissus love affair I thought was behind me for another year. An incredibly elegant *Narcissus*, its petals – which are crinkled and ever so slightly recurved at the tips – are held on mid-green stems that emerge from a mass of floaty, strap-like leaves in a kind of olive-green. They glisten like fresh snow, and it is hard to think of any other flower that is quite as brilliant white as this all year. At the centre, the sterility is broken by a short corona in a mustard shade of yellow that is edged, quite astonishingly, with the hottest lick of vermillion.

Planting note: *Narcissus poeticus* var. *recurvus* should be thought of in terms of an early summer planting scheme, as opposed to spring when the rest of their peers are flowering. They combine well with bearded irises (*Iris germanica*) and alliums to create a glorious melee of colour and texture.

Orlaya grandiflora (white laceflower)

Annual • Summer • Height: up to 70cm (28in), spread: up to 50cm (20in) • Full sun • All soil types except very heavy clay • Vase life: good (up to 1 week) • Flower colour value: light

Orlaya grandiflora is a sophisticated annual that adds a touch of elegance to a planting scheme or cut flower display. The long stems hold saucer-shaped flowers that sway pleasantly in the wind like a hovering butterfly looking for the perfect bloom upon which to land. For a flower so unassuming, its shape is intriguingly complex, with concentric circles of flat umbels that are significantly larger on the outside than those found towards the centre. The stamens are creamy, but each petal is a pure, brilliant white.

Planting note: The performance of *Orlaya grandiflora* can be prolonged by regular deadheading, and, in my experience, it can certainly be considered as a cut-and-come again annual. The more that is harvested for the house, the more it blooms in the garden.

Beyond Reflection

The tranquillity of reflective greens, blues and whites feels so perfectly melodic that often it is hard to conceive how this palette could be bettered (indeed, to my mind, in many ways it cannot). These colours share a certain basic and instinctive purity with which little else can compete. However, with a garden so full of colour opportunity there is an endless temptation to experiment.

Dark purple

Brooding dark purple brings a mysterious quality to whites, greens and blues – an added depth that increases the complexity of the palette. It is the kind of purple that in dull conditions appears suspiciously black, but when illuminated by the brilliant light of a clear summer's day transforms into a sparkling magenta – *Scabiosa atropurpurea* 'Black Knight', *Tulipa* 'Continental' and the sweet pea *Lathyrus odoratus* 'Beaujolais' are striking examples. Against the neutrality of white and the passivity of green, this is a colour that frames; its shadows echoing through its more luminous counterparts. When paired with blue, it adds a sumptuous and luxurious feel to the display, as though peering inside a shimmering box of jewels.

Bright yellow

Sunshine-yellows have an inherent simplicity that pairs well with the clarity of a reflective palette. With white, bright yellows feel fresh and invigorating; it is a spring display of pearly *Narcissus* 'Elka' mixed through the glorious sparkle of 'Eaton Song' or, in late summer, *Cosmos bipinnatus* 'Purity' floating through *Rudbeckia fulgida* var. *sullivantii* 'Goldsturm'. Together they have a certain rawness that feels clean and uncomplicated. Paired with mid- to dark greens, bright yellows mimic the effect of chartreuse; they create a sense of acidity, an electric current running through the composition. In the spring garden, it could be *Crocus* × *luteus* 'Golden Yellow' dotted between the handsome leaves of hellebores. In the vase, it might be a simple display of fennel (*Foeniculum vulgare*) bouncing through summer foliage.

Oppositge: Greens, whites and blues are punctuated with shades of yellows from *Achillea* 'Coronation Gold', St John's wort (*Hypericum perforatum*) and marigolds (*Calendula*). The result is a thrilling explosion of colour that, although lively, retains a calming sense of tranquillity.

Illustrative Reflective Planting Plan

Delphinium Black Knight Group and *Angelica archangelica* anchor this reflective planting plan. The contrast in their colouring and values – delphinium in a dark electric blue, angelica in a light green-ivory – makes them a compelling pairing as the key focal points in the composition.

Baltic parsley (*Cenolophium denudatum*), an umbellifer with billowing clouds of pearl-white flowers, drifts through the composition, encouraging the eye to travel through the entirety of the planting scheme. At the centre there are instances of Turkish sage (*Phlomis russeliana*), which, with their lemon-yellow flowers, offer moments that break from the blue-green-white palette and in turn give the eye a reference point to which it can periodically return.

Appearing on both sides, *Dahlia* 'Bishop of Dover' frames the scheme with creamy, star-shaped flowers, which are intensified by the darkness of its foliage. Beneath these dahlias, an understorey of texture from the chartreuse of lady's mantle (*Alchemilla mollis*) and the powdery blue of *Geranium* Rozanne creeps through moments of white laceflower (*Orlaya grandiflora*) and the elegant *Astrantia major* 'Alba'.

Overall, there is a calming sense of looseness; the planting appears untethered, floating effortlessly in and out of itself.

But with a scheme as muted and restrained as this, it is key that colour is not solely relied upon to bring interest. In this plan, a sense of dynamism is created in the rise and fall of planting at different heights, and this picks up any visual slack that might be lost in the foregoing of a more vibrant palette. Similarly, a mix of textures – ethereal umbellifers alongside leafy *Alchemilla mollis* and hardy geraniums, upright and architectural *Angelica archangelica* neighbouring the fragility of *Orlaya grandiflora* – stops the eye from becoming lost in a monotonous carpet of neutral colour and, in turn, prevents any feeling of boredom.

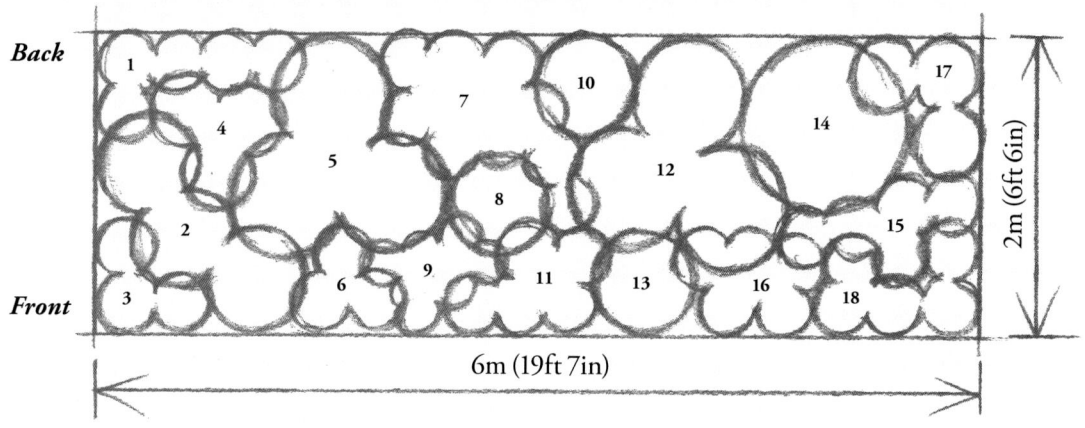

Scale: 1:50

1. *Cenolophium denudatum* × 5
2. *Geranium* Rozanne × 3
3. *Alchemilla mollis* × 3
4. *Dahlia* 'Bishop of Dover' × 3
5. *Delphinium* Black Knight Group × 3
6. *Astrantia major* 'Alba' × 3
7. *Cenolophium denudatum* × 11
8. *Phlomis russeliana* × 1
9. *Orlaya grandiflora* × 7
10. *Phlomis russeliana* × 1
11. *Alchemilla mollis* × 5
12. *Delphinium* Black Knight Group × 3
13. *Phlomis russeliana* × 1
14. *Angelica archangelica* × 1
15. *Cenolophium denudatum* × 5
16. *Astrantia major* 'Alba' × 5
17. *Dahlia* 'Bishop of Dover' × 3
18. *Alchemilla mollis* × 5

Notes

This illustrative planting plan would reach its peak in mid-summer and perform best in full sun. Its season of interest could be extended by scattering through spring bulbs such as old pheasan't eye (*Narcissus poeticus* var. *recurvus*), *Tulipa* 'Spring Green', ox-eye daisy (*Leucanthemum vulgare*) and *Muscari* 'Peppermint'.

Notes on
Reflective Cut Flower Displays

Reflective indoor displays place as much emphasis on foliage as they do flowers. Mixing a variety of leaf shapes and grasses with loose and informal blooms creates floating, ethereal arrangements that emit a soft sense of tranquillity. It might be the frilly, disc-shaped foliage of lady's mantle (*Alchemilla mollis*) or the spent flower heads of hellebores and *Euphorbia amygdaloides* var. *robbiae*. Either way, these moments of texture help to bring a true sense of the garden's calming tapestry inside.

I am always looking to create a sense of space with reflective displays, a feeling of the flowers loosely exploring their surroundings. Flower frogs and chicken wire help to secure the largest stems in place – perhaps clouds of Baltic parsley (*Cenolophium denudatum*) or wafting spires of white-flowered foxglove (*Digitalis purpurea* f. *albiflora*) – but these mechanics are only used lightly to keep the arrangement as unfettered as possible.

Opposite: Delphiniums, geraniums and lady's mantle (*Alchemilla mollis*) in the cloisters at Iford Manor, Wiltshire. Above left: A soothing display of *Narcissus* 'Tommy White', lily of the valley (*Convallaria majalis*) and cow parsley (*Anthriscus sylvestris*). Above right: A handful of lady's mantle and cornflowers (*Centaurea cyanus*).

When it is a sense of calm that is desired, I think it is important to allow the flowers to wander freely through the display.

Light plays an important role. There is something so incredibly soothing in the way a soft, golden evening glow descends upon a display of flowers in the house, a magic that I am forever looking to capture by placing displays on the windowsills of my cottage. It is often worthwhile thinking about those flowers that really exploit this type of light and transform into illuminated stained glass under its influence. The likes of ivory daffodils (*Narcissus* 'Mount Hood', 'Elka'), buttery *Cosmos bipinnatus* ('Xanthos', 'Lemonade'), translucent sweet peas (*Lathyrus odoratus* 'Castle of Mey', 'Juliet') and frothy thalictrum ('Elin', *Thalictrum pubescens*) are good examples; flowers that at any other time are muted and demure, but have the ability, under the sparkle of a setting sun, to reflect light like a disco ball.

A reflective arrangement of flowers is elevated by the introduction of scent. Drifts of floral perfume capture an abstract, other-worldly feeling; it is as though these scents belong to a different realm – somewhere enchanted – and by some kind of magic their echoes have found themselves meandering through the house. This is highly calming to me. These scents take my mind away from the everyday and give fuel to my imagination. The best displays catch you off-guard: a moment walking through the hallway suddenly interrupted by a hit of sweet pea perfume, settling down to sleep as a surprising, fruity ripple of honeysuckle floats by.

I am often keen to keep vessels as unfussy as possible when the objective of a display is to soothe – the more basic, the better. Perhaps it is simple jam jars, a plain jug or unelaborate glass bud vases. Either way, it is important to me that the focus remains on the flowers; ultimately, it is they that hold the power to calm.

Right: A selection of garden roses in candied pinks, buttery yellows and creamy ivory on the garden table.

ATMOSPHERE 3: REFLECTIVE

Atmosfloric:

Escaping with Flower Colour

Romance, energy and reflection: three floral atmospheres that speak to our constant search for escape. In lives that are busied by the never-ending demands of deadlines and made fraught by the uncertainty of a hostile world, gardens and cut flower displays offer a gentle distraction. They bring our minds back to the simple and effortless beauty of nature, moments that demand nothing from us, except an ability to exist entirely in the present.

When I walk through a garden in early summer that is powdered by the dusky pinks of roses, bearded irises, foxgloves, lupins and alliums, the sense of romance I feel is all-encompassing. When I put together a simple display of cut flowers in early autumn that is set alight by the burning reds and oranges of crocosmia, heleniums and dahlias, the energy that I take from it is limitless. When in winter I look out onto hedgerows carpeted by pearly white snowdrops, the feeling of calm is absolute. These colours, born from the magic of nature, have an unparalleled ability to take me away from the troubles and messy complications of day-to-day life. For a moment I am nowhere else; I am rooted wholly in the majesty of the here and now.

It is an atmosfloric world and there is a deep joy in finding your place within it. Over years of gardening and creating cut flower displays, I have come to find the colour ingredients that best capture my imagination (hopefully, I have successfully illustrated them in this book), but part of what makes us so interesting as people is the varied ways in which we interpret and interact with the environment around us. Throughout these pages we have seen how floral atmosphere and mood is approached in different ways. There is the romantic assemblage of textures created at Charleston and in the homes of Marin Montagut, Sam McKnight and Beth Tarling, places where colour is used to soften the harshness of modern life and offer an escape into a whimsical world made more poetic. There is the highly energetic layering of objects at the homes of Richard E. Grant, Robin Lucas, Isabel and Julian Bannerman, and Max Hurd. Idiosyncratic spaces that use colour to inspire, motivate and ignite a certain sparkle within those who live there. And also, the soothing gracefulness of Kettle's Yard, Perrycroft, Atelier Vime, and the home of Butter Wakefield: cocoons of calm where colour washes through like a comforting blanket of tranquillity. All these people have carved out their own relationship with flower colour. They use it thoughtfully to enhance the kind of atmosphere that resonates most profoundly with them.

Opposite, top from left: Foxgloves (*Digitalis purpurea*) in the cottage garden; *Hippeastrum* 'Wild Amazone'; *Digitalis purpurea* f. *albiflora*. Middle row, from left: Deadheading dahlias and rudbeckias in late summer; delphiniums and love-in-a-mist (*Nigella damascena* 'Miss Jekyll'); *Tulipa* 'Chansonnette'. Bottom row, from left: A chartreuse display of euphorbia in early spring; a fountain of tulips in spring; *Dahlia* 'Maldini'.

In so doing, these home owners have created intimate sanctuaries that offer little windows into the world of their imagination.

Finding a personal way with flower colour is an evolving pastime, a never-ending experiment. Year after year, season after season, the continued layering of tints, tones and shades in both the garden and the vase, so that the result is meaningful in some way, consumes an inordinate amount of my time. It is the thrill of discovering a new variety of sweet pea or acquiring a new rose, the sudden rush of excitement browsing seeds or visiting a plant nursery. A universe of colour possibility is unlocked within me.

There will be readers of this book looking for advice on how to be more adventurous with flower colour. People for whom the endless choice of tints, tones and shades is perhaps more daunting than it is exciting. My advice is, hopefully, simple. Instead of viewing colour as something immediate and tangible, begin to shift your thinking so that, instead, it is seen as more of an emotion. On the surface, a bright yellow rudbeckia (perhaps *Rudbeckia hirta* 'Prairie Sun') is just that: bright. It presents itself with a certain tenacity that can be off-putting to those who naturally lean towards more subtle and nuanced expressions of colour. But stick with it for a moment. What if underneath the brashness was a suggestion of something more charismatic? Its canary-yellow petals, far from being vulgar, are really the echoes of a perfect summer's evening; a time just before twilight when the sun seems to illuminate the landscape most intensely and everything is suddenly imbued with simple lucidity. Or perhaps they represent the meeting of lovers under lemon trees somewhere by the Italian coast? Maybe they symbolize the innocence of youth? By looking deeper – getting under the skin of different hues – there is the opportunity to write our own stories and to make sense of the thoughts and feelings that move us in some way. It is about cultivating a connection with colour, a certain respect perhaps, that runs deeper than the superficial. Exploring the opportunities they give to us for self-discovery.

A flower farmer not far from where I live in Somerset, Sarah Wilson, is someone who shares this passion for colour investigation. I am a regular visitor to her plot, and our conversations about the current joys and frustrations with the flowers we grow is often as fulfilling as the blooms I take away with me. On a visit recently, we found ourselves enthralled by the deep raspberry-red of a sweet William (the cultivar was *Dianthus barbatus* 'Electron'), and both of us remarked on the sense of energetic vitality it created next to the sunset-orange of the marigold *Calendula officinalis* 'Neon'. As Sarah told me: 'Sometimes it is not the flowers themselves, but the colours that grow in this field that really excites me. The way they speak to each other. That is the quiet satisfaction of this work.'

Quiet satisfaction. I cannot think of a better way of describing my relationship with flower colour. When I am selecting a tint, tone or shade for the garden or the vase, there is an inward sense of self-reflection (and, in many ways, self-indulgence). I am lost to dreamlands that exist only in my mind, creating love stories out of pastels and dramas out of brights. I suppose hidden within everything I create is a kind of scrapbook of thoughts and feelings. A pink that reminds me of something sweet from childhood or an orange that inspires future plans. I can see my whole life and everything I am still yet to achieve in the kaleidoscope of pigments that the garden produces. These colours are more than just decorative to me; they are a personal story. Part autobiography, part fantasy.

Opposite, top row from left: A display of *Oenothera lindheimeri* Geyser Pink; snowdrops (*Galanthus nivalis*); buttery roses in Sam McKnight's garden. Middle row, from left: Energetic tulips in spring; dahlias and zinnias in late summer; English bluebells (*Hyacinthoides non-scripta*). Bottom row, from left: Rosa mundi (*Rosa gallica* 'Versicolor'); an early spring display of daffodils; high summer garden table.

Index

Achillea 16, 86, 208
Agapanthus 16, 147–9, 198
Alcea rosea (hollyhocks) 42, 64, 75
Alchemilla mollis 11, 18, 20–1, 24, 78–81, 88, 90–1, 125, 128, 134–7, 140, 146, 164, 175, 178, 181, 187, 195, 202–3, 210–11, 213
Allium 17, 21, 42, 85, 134, 136–7, 140, 167, 170, 198–9, 207, 217
Ammi majus 28, 150, 164, 178, 189, 206
analogous colours 23
Anemone coronaria 16, 135, 137, 150, 203
  A. x *hybrida* 'Robustissima' 80, 90–1
Angelica 18, 78–9, 81, 202, 210–11
Anthriscus sylvestris 39, 156, 213
Antirrhinum majus (snapdragons) 69
Aquilegia 'Rose Queen' 170
  A. chrysantha 'Yellow Queen' 140, 170
Archer, Gillian 175–8
Asplenium trichomanes 80
Aster x *frikartii* 'Mönch' 24, 75, 147–8, 156
Astilbe 86, 136
Astrantia 32, 80, 150, 210–11
  A. major 'Star of Love' 80
Atelier Vime, France 189–92, 217
atmosphere 37, 217–18
  energetic 97, 99–100, 105–9, 111–14, 119–22, 125–8
  reflective 159, 161–2, 167–70, 175–8, 181–4, 189–92
  romantic 39, 41–3, 47–50, 53–6, 61–4, 69–72

Background 31
Bannerman, Isabel and Julian 18, 111–14, 217
Bistorta amplexicaulis 'Fat Domino' 81, 134
blue 88, 150, 197–9
Brugmansia suaveolens 114
Bupleurum griffithii 164

Calamagrostis x *acutiflora* 152–3
Calendula officinalis 5, 16–17, 69, 72, 122, 142, 147–9, 155, 198–9, 208, 218
Camassia leichtlinii 149
Campanula poscharskyana 11
Cenolophium denudatum (Baltic parsley) 28, 146, 150, 152–3, 206, 210–11, 213

Centaurea cyanus 11, 21, 24, 125, 127, 148, 164, 195, 198, 213
Centranthus (valerian) 39, 77, 136
  C. ruber 'Roseus' 136
Charleston, East Sussex 5, 31, 61–4, 217
clematis 81, 143
colour preferences 27
colour temperature 34
colour value 34
colour wheel 14–24
complementary colours 20–1
Convallaria (lily of the valley) 23, 213
Cosmos 18, 24, 32–4, 69, 81, 114, 134–6, 189, 192, 208
  C. atrosanguineus Cherry Chocolate 33, 134, 136
  C. bipinnatus 'Candy Floss Pink Sunrise' 78, 87, 90–1
  C. b. 'Xanthos' 21, 28, 32, 87, 142, 152–3, 214
Crocosmia 17–18, 50, 150, 201, 217
  C. x *crocosmiiflora* 'Emily McKenzie' 24, 140, 147, 148, 152–3
Crocus 18, 83–4, 100, 135, 139, 150, 208
  C. tommasinianus 84, 143

Daffodils 20, 27, 33, 64, 83, 95, 100, 103, 139, 141, 150, 153, 154, 214, 218, 223
  see also Narcissus
Dahlia 8, 13, 21, 23–4, 32, 37, 41, 69, 72, 75, 78, 80–1, 103, 111, 119, 121–2, 131, 142, 146–9, 152–5, 161, 184, 210–11, 217–18, 223
  D. 'Arabian Night' 93, 136, 137, 152–3
  D. 'Bishop of Auckland' 122, 134, 152–3
  D. 'Bishop of York' 23, 87, 137, 140, 152–3
  D. 'Maldini' 81, 217
Delphinium 8, 18, 23, 109, 146–7, 164, 184, 210–11, 213, 217
Dianthus barbatus 'Electron Mix' 137, 218
Digitalis (foxgloves) 18, 21, 39, 42, 75, 80, 85, 146–7, 150, 162, 168, 199, 202, 213, 217
Dipsacus fullorum 17
Dryopteris affinis 'Cristata' 80

Echinacea 18, 21, 78, 80–1, 100, 134–7
Echinops 18, 81, 148
energetic flower colour 131

beyond energy 150
cut flower displays 154–5
illustrative planting plan 152–3
orange 145–9
red 133–7
yellow 139–43
Epimedium 80
  E. x *versicolor* 'Sulphureum' 141, 142
Erigeron karvinskianus 11, 39, 168
Erysimum cheiri 135, 142–3, 149
Eschscholzia californica 146, 198
Euphorbia 20, 23, 79–81, 88, 134–7, 201, 203, 213, 217
  E. amygdaloides var. *robbiae* 203

Fennel (*Foeniculum vulgare*) 121–2, 208
ferns 50, 80, 100, 140, 170, 203
Filipendula rubra 'Venusta' 80
Fritillaria imperialis 149, 154
  F. meleagris 79, 84, 141–2, 150, 161

Galanthus (snowdrops) 109, 184, 205, 217–18
Geranium 17, 20–1, 23–4, 34, 42, 50, 75, 78–9, 85, 88, 90–2, 143, 147, 198–9, 202, 206, 210–11, 213
  G. Rozanne 198
Geum 18, 24, 50, 137, 150, 153, 198–9, 202–3
Gladiolus communis 81
Grant, Richard E. 125–8, 217
green 88, 201–3

Helenium 114, 140, 147–8, 150, 217
Helianthus 72, 122, 146, 150, 155, 189, 192
Helleborus 79, 84, 86–7, 135
Heuchera 'Fireworks' 199
Hippeastrum 'Wild Amazone' 217
Hosta 17, 201, 203
Hurd, Max 105–9, 217
Hyacinthoides non-scripta 148, 197, 218
Hyacinthus 16, 18, 141–2, 146, 149–50, 154, 161
hydrangeas 75
Hypericum perforatum 164, 208

Iris 17–18, 21, 23, 39, 42–3, 56, 75, 79, 83–8, 90–2, 109, 140–3, 152–4, 197–9, 202–3, 206–7, 217
  I. 'Grand Chief' 146, 152–3
  I. 'Prince of Burgundy' 85

I. orientalis 42, 206
I. reticulata 83–4, 187
I. x *robusta* 'Gerald Darby' 199

Jasmine 81, 143

Kettle's Yard, Cambridge 13, 181–4, 217
Kniphofia 'Sunningdale Yellow' 177

Lathyrus odoratus 18, 21, 28, 69, 78, 80, 137, 142–3, 146, 155, 195, 199
   L. odoratus 'Beaujolais' 32–3, 86, 208
   L. odoratus 'Winston Churchill' 134
Leucanthemum vulgare 32, 211
light 32–3
lilies 75, 119, 146, 154
Lilium 'Tiger Babies' 146
   L. leichtlinii 122
   L. regale 79
Lucas, Robin 119–22, 217
Lunaria annua (honesty) 141, 150, 203
Lupinus 81, 85, 147, 150, 198, 217
Luzula nivea 202

Malva trimestris 'Mont Blanc' 28
McKnight, Sam, MBE 47–50, 53, 217, 218
Molinia caerulea 78
Moluccella laevis 17, 81, 134, 137, 178
Monarda 'Cambridge Scarlet' 16, 20, 28, 80, 150, 152–3
Montagut, Marin 53–6, 217
Muscari (grape hyacinth) 20–1, 79, 84, 87–8, 135, 149–50, 192, 211
Myosotis (forget-me-nots) 42, 50, 146

Narcissus 5, 18, 21, 23, 28, 31, 32, 61, 62, 84, 86, 135, 141–3, 155, 162, 203, 207–8, 211, 213
   N. bulbocodium 'Arctic Bells' 142
   N. poeticus var. *recurvus* 162, 207, 211
   see also daffodils
Nepeta 23, 32, 79, 85–7, 143, 199, 206
Nicotiana langsdorfii 78, 80, 136, 202–3
Nigella damascena 43, 125, 198–9
   N. d. 'Miss Jekyll' 8, 21, 128, 146, 149, 199, 217

Oenothera lindheimeri 136
   O. l. 'Geyser Pink' 78, 90–1, 134
orange 145–9
orchid, common spotted 178

Orlaya grandiflora 207, 210–11
Osmanthus x *burkwoodii* 170

Pelargoniums 41, 69, 72, 114, 119
Pennisetum advena 'Rubrum' 80, 134
Penstemon 21, 77–8, 87, 142, 150, 202
peonies 187
Phacelia campanularia 16, 198, 202
Phlomis russelliana 86, 143, 198, 210–11
phlox 28, 77, 114, 119, 175, 177
pink 77–81
Polygonatum x *hybridum* (Solomon's Seal) 50, 100, 154, 203
poppy (*Oreomecon*) 13, 100, 184
poppy (*Papaver*) 16, 21, 24, 77, 105, 137, 201, 203
primary colours 16
Primula 'Silver Lace Black' 86
   P. auricula 86
   P. veris (cowslips) 16, 84–7, 139, 150
   P. vulgaris (primroses) 84, 100, 139, 150, 162, 184
purple 83–7, 150, 208

Red 133–7
reflective flower colour 195
   beyond reflection 208
   blue 197–9
   cut flower displays 213–14
   green 201–3
   illustrative planting plan 210–11
   white 205–7
romantic flower colour 75
   beyond romanticism 88
   cut flower displays 92–3
   illustrative planting plan 90–1
   pink 77–81
   purple 83–7
Rosa 21, 28, 43, 47, 50, 75, 77–80, 142–3, 146–7, 175, 202, 218
   R. 'Albertine' 42, 77, 81, 136
   R. 'Emily Gray' 42, 143
   R. Boscobel ('Auscousin') 23–4, 42–3, 77, 79, 85, 90–1, 93, 127
   R. Lady of Shalott ('Ausnyson') 18, 55, 140, 147, 198
   R. Munstead Wood ('Ausbernard') 23, 85–6, 90–1, 142, 198
Rudbeckia 37, 103, 114, 145, 147–8, 208, 217–18

R. hirta 'Autumn Colours' 24, 134, 147, 152–3

Salvia 21 32, 50, 64, 75, 78, 81, 87, 91, 114, 136, 140, 147, 148–9, 198–9, 202
Sanguisorba hakusanensis 81
Scabiosa 24, 69, 199
   S. atropurpurea 'Black Knight' 21, 83, 87, 90–1, 140, 208
Scilla 20, 84, 197
secondary colours 17
Silene coronaria 18, 23, 199
Symphyotrichum novae-angliae 137

Tagetes patula 99, 111, 114
   T. p. 'Burning Embers' 21, 103, 135
Tanacetum parthenium (feverfew) 28, 175
Tarling, Beth 69–72, 217
tertiary colours 18
tetradic colours 24
Thalictrum 77, 214
Tiarella 79, 87, 135
Tithonia rotundifolia 'Torch' 17, 24, 114, 134, 148, 152–3
Tropaeolum majus (nasturtiums) 99–100, 122, 131, 145, 154–5
   T. m. 'Jewel of Africa' 148, 149, 198
Tulipa 8, 11, 18, 20–1, 23–4, 32, 37, 41, 50, 53, 58, 64, 79, 83–4, 86–8, 99–100, 131, 141, 149–50, 153–5, 159, 162, 170, 184, 203, 207–8, 211, 217–18
   T. 'Ballerina' 149, 153
   T. 'Columbus' 79, 86, 91
   T. 'Continental' 32, 34, 87, 91, 93, 208
   T. 'Couleur Cardinal' 20, 34, 135, 163
   T. turkestanica 143

Verbascum chaixi 'Album' 177
Verbena bonariensis 90–1, 137, 140, 150, 152–3
Viola 154
   V. x *wittrockiana* 'Frizzle Sizzle Yellow-blue Swirl' 141

Wakefield, Butter 167–70, 217
white 28, 150, 205–7

Yellow 88, 139–43, 208

Zinnia 13, 24, 27, 37, 69, 78, 80, 88, 99, 103, 111, 116, 131, 134–7, 184, 201, 218

Acknowledgements

A very special thank you to everybody who has helped bring this book to life, particularly the featured homeowners and all those behind-the-scenes at the cultural institutions that have been included. All have not only been so generous with their time and enthusiasm for this project, but also endless in their hospitality and patience. Without you, there would be no book at all!

A heartfelt thanks must also go to the team at Mitchell Beazley (Alison, Jonathan, Liz, Sybella, Caroline, Vik and Charlotte), who put their faith in me and this project, and have once again been a complete delight to work with.

And, as ever, thank you to Dan for keeping me going through the many periods of self-doubt.

With endless gratitude also to: Alice Boissonnet (Du Vent dans les Bottes), Anna (Anna's Flower Farm), Anthony Watson and Benoît Rauzy (Atelier Vime), Beth and Dan Tarling, Butter Wakefield, Elizabeth Wilkinson (Kettle's Yard), Emerald Brown (ODD), Gillian and Mark Archer (Perrycroft), Helen and Paul Stickland (Blackshed Flowers), Isabel and Julian Bannerman, Jenny Parkinson (PA to Sam McKnight), Karen Fielding (The Natural Flower Field Company), Kathy Crisp (Conservator at Charleston), Leah Dennison (Charleston), Marianne and William Cartwright-Hignett (Iford Manor), Marie Varenne (Fleurs d'Arles), Marin Montagut and Alexis Gilot, Martin Clark (Tilley Printing), Max Hurd, Phoebe Clive (Tinsmiths), Richard E. Grant, Robin Lucas and Tom, Rozanne Delamore (Ledbury Flower Farmer), Sam McKnight, Sarah Wilson (Compton Garden Flowers), Steve Lannin (Iford Manor), Treea Cracknell (The London Flower Farmer).

First published in Great Britain in 2026 by
Mitchell Beazley, an imprint of
Octopus Publishing Group Ltd, Carmelite House,
50 Victoria Embankment, London EC4Y 0DZ
www.octopusbooks.co.uk

An Hachette UK Company
www.hachette.co.uk

The authorized representative in the EEA is Hachette Ireland, 8 Castlecourt Centre, Dublin 15, D15 XTP3, Ireland (email: info@hbgi.ie)

Text, photography and illustrations copyright © Sean A. Pritchard 2026

Distributed in the US by Hachette Book Group, 1290 Avenue of the Americas, 4th and 5th Floors, New York, NY 10104

Distributed in Canada by Canadian Manda Group, 664 Annette St., Toronto, Ontario, Canada M6S 2C8

All rights reserved. No part of this work may be reproduced or utilized in any form or by any means, electronic or mechanical, including photocopying, recording or by any information storage and retrieval system, without the prior written permission of the publisher.

Sean A. Pritchard has asserted their right under the Copyright, Designs and Patents Act 1988 to be identified as the author of this work.

ISBN: 978 1 84091 935 6
eISBN: 978 1 84091 937 0

A CIP catalogue record for this book is available from the British Library.

Printed and bound in China.

10 9 8 7 6 5 4 3 2 1

Publishing Director: Alison Starling
Senior Managing Editor: Sybella Stephens
Copy Editor: Caroline West
Creative Director: Jonathan Christie
Senior Production Manager: Katherine Hockley

Opposite: Single stems of dahlias, in a soothing creamy ivory, by a window at my cottage.

Page 224: A playful and highly energetic display of forced rhubarb and daffodils in early spring.

Sean A Pritchard has a garden design studio based in London and Somerset. He came to his career in garden design with a background in fine art and brand strategy. Before setting up his design practice, Sean graduated with Distinction from the Garden Design School in Bristol. Sean has designed show gardens at RHS Hampton Court Palace Garden Festival and, in 2025, he designed The ODD Pavilion at RHS Chelsea Flower Show. He divides his time between London and Somerset, where he lives in a 300-year-old farm labourer's cottage on the Mendip Hills, overlooking the Somerset Levels. He applies much of his garden design philosophy to the decoration of his cottage, which he shares on his popular Instagram account, @sean_anthony_pritchard His first book *Outside In* was published by Mitchell Beazley in 2024.